Expelled from Spain

Jacques Casanova de Seingalt

[ZHINGOORA BOOKS]

EXPELLED FROM SPAIN

CHAPTER VII

I Make a Mistake and Manucci Becomes My Mortal Foe—His Vengeance—I Leave Madrid—Saragossa—Valentia—Nina—I Arrive at Barcelona

If these Memoirs, only written to console me in the dreadful weariness which is slowly killing me in Bohemia—and which, perhaps, would kill me anywhere, since, though my body is old, my spirit and my desires are as young as ever—if these Memoirs are ever read, I repeat, they will only be read when I am gone, and all censure will be lost on me.

Nevertheless, seeing that men are divided into two sections, the one and by far the greater composed of the ignorant and superficial, and the other of the learned and reflective, I beg to state that it is to the latter I would appeal. Their judgment, I believe, will be in favour of my veracity, and, indeed, why should I not be veracious? A man can have no object in deceiving himself, and it is for myself that I chiefly write.

Hitherto I have spoken nothing but the truth, without considering whether the truth is in my favour or no. My book is not a work of dogmatic theology, but I do not think it will do harm to anyone; while I fancy that those who know how to imitate the bee and to get honey from every flower will be able to extract some good from the catalogue of my vices and virtues.

After this digression (it may be too long, but that is my business and none other's), I must confess that never have I had so unpleasant a truth to set down as that which I am going to relate. I committed a fatal act of indiscretion—an act which after all these years still gives my heart a pang as I think of it.

The day after my conquest I dined with the Venetian ambassador, and I had the pleasure of hearing that all the ministers and grandees with whom I had associated had the highest possible opinion of me. In three or four days the king, the royal family, and the ministers would return to town, and I expected to have daily conferences with the latter respecting the colony in the Sierra Morena, where I should most probably be going. Manucci, who continued to treat me as a valued friend, proposed to accompany me on my journey, and would bring with him an adventuress, who called herself Porto-Carrero, pretending to be the daughter or niece of the late cardinal of that name, and thus obtained a good deal of consideration; though in reality she was only the mistress of the French consul at Madrid, the Abbe Bigliardi.

Such was the promising state of my prospects when my evil genius brought to Madrid a native of Liege, Baron de Fraiture, chief huntsman of the principality, and a profligate, a gamester, and a cheat, like all those who proclaim their belief in his honesty nowadays.

I had unfortunately met him at Spa, and told him I was was going to Portugal. He had come after me, hoping to use me as a means of getting into good society, and of filling his pocket with the money of the dupes he aspired to make.

Gamesters have never had any proof of my belonging to their infernal clique, but they have always persisted in believing that I too am a "Greek."

As soon as this baron heard that I was in Madrid he called on me, and by dint of politeness obliged me to receive him. I thought any small civilities I might shew or introductions I might give could do me no harm. He had a travelling companion to whom he introduced me. He was a fat, ignorant fellow, but a Frenchman, and therefore agreeable. A Frenchman who knows how to present himself, who is well dressed, and has the society air, is usually accepted without demur or scrutiny. He had been a cavalry captain, but had been fortunate enough to obtain an everlasting furlough.

Four or five days after his appearance the baron asked me quietly enough to lend him a score of louis, as he was hard up. I replied as quietly, thanking him for treating me as a friend, but informing him that I really could not lend him the money, as I wanted what little I had for my own necessities.

"But we can do good business together, and you cannot possibly be moneyless."

"I do not know anything about good business, but I do know that I want my money and cannot part with it."

"We are at our wits' end to quiet our landlord; come and speak to him."

"If I were to do so I should do you more harm than good. He would ask me if I would answer for you, and I should reply that you are one of those noblemen who stand in need of no surety. All the same, the landlord would think that if I did not stand your surety, it must be from my entertaining doubts as to your solvency."

I had introduced Fraiture to Count Manucci, on the Pando, and he requested me to take him to see the count, to which request I was foolish enough to accede.

A few days later the baron opened his soul to Manucci.

He found the Venetian disposed to be obliging, but wary. He refused to lend money himself, but introduced the baron to someone who lent him money on pledges without interest.

The baron and his friend did a little gaming and won a little money, but I held aloof from them to the best of my ability.

I had my colony and Donna Ignazia, and wanted to live peacefully; and if I had spent a single night away from home, the innocent girl would have been filled with alarm.

About that time M. de Mocenigo went as ambassador to France, and was replaced by M. Querini. Querini was a man of letters, while Mocenigo only liked music and his own peculiar kind of love.

The new ambassador was distinctly favourable to me, and in a few days I had reason to believe that he would do more for me than ever Mocenigo would have done.

In the meanwhile, the baron and his friend began to think of beating a retreat to France. There was no gaming at the ambassador's and no gaming at the Court; they must return to France, but they owed money to their landlord, and they wanted money for the journey. I could give them nothing, Manucci would give them nothing; we both pitied them, but our duty to ourselves made us cruel to everyone else. However, he brought trouble on us.

One morning Manucci came to see me in evident perturbation.

"What is the matter?" said I.

"I do not know exactly. For the last week I have refused to see the Baron Fraiture, as not being able to give him money, his presence only wearied me. He has written me a letter, in which he threatens to blow out his brains to-day if I will not lend him a hundred pistoles."

"He said the same thing to me three days ago; but I replied that I would bet two hundred pistoles that he would do nothing of the kind. This made him angry, and he proposed to fight a duel with me; but I declined on the plea that as he was a desperate man either he would have an advantage over me or I, over him. Give him the same answer, or, better still, no answer at all."

"I cannot follow your advice. Here are the hundred pistoles. Take them to him and get a receipt."

I admired his generosity and agreed to carry out his commission. I called on the baron, who seemed rather uncomfortable when I walked in; but considering his position I was not at all surprised.

I informed him that I was the bearer of a thousand francs from Count Manucci, who thereby placed him in a position to arrange his affairs and to leave Madrid. He received the money without any signs of pleasure, surprise, or gratitude, and wrote out the receipt. He assured me that he and his friend would start for Barcelona and France on the following day.

I then took the document to Manucci, who was evidently suffering from some mental trouble; and I remained to dinner with the ambassador. It was for the last time.

Three days after I went to dine with the ambassadors (for they all dined together), but to my astonishment the porter told me that he had received orders not to admit me.

The effect of this sentence on me was like that of a thunderbolt; I returned home like a man in a dream. I immediately sat down and wrote to Manucci, asking him why I had been subjected to such an insult; but Philippe, my man, brought me back the letter unopened.

This was another surprise; I did not know what to expect next. "What can be the matter?" I said to myself. "I cannot imagine, but I will have an explanation, or perish."

I dined sadly with Donna Ignazia, without telling her the cause of my trouble, and just as I was going to take my siesta a servant of Manucci's brought me a letter from his master and fled before I could read it. The letter contained an enclosure which I read first. It was from Baron de Fraiture. He asked Manucci to lend him a hundred pistoles, promising to shew him the man whom he held for his dearest friend to be his worst enemy.

Manucci (honouring me, by the way, with the title of ungrateful traitor) said that the baron's letter had excited his curiosity and he had met him in St. Jerome's Park, where the baron had clearly proved this enemy to be myself, since I had informed the baron that though the name of Manucci was genuine the title of count was quite apocryphal.

After recapitulating the information which Fraiture had given him, and which could only have proceeded from myself, he advised me to leave Madrid as soon as possible, in a week at latest.

I can give the reader no idea of the shock this letter gave me. For the first time in my life I had to confess myself guilty of folly, ingratitude, and crime. I felt that my fault was beyond forgiveness, and did not think of asking Manucci to pardon me; I could do nothing but despair.

Nevertheless, in spite of Manucci's just indignation, I could not help seeing that he had made a great mistake in advising me, in so insulting a manner, to leave Madrid in a week. The young man might have known that my self-respect would forbid my following such a piece of advice. He could not compel me to obey his counsel or command; and to leave Madrid would have been to commit a second baseness worse than the first.

A prey to grief I spent the day without taking any steps one way or the other, and I went to bed without supping and without the company of Donna Ignazia.

After a sound sleep I got up and wrote to the friend whom I had offended a sincere and humble confession of my fault. I concluded my letter by saying that I hoped that this evidence of my sincere and heartfelt repentance would suffice, but if not that I was ready to give him any honourable satisfaction in my power.

"You may," I said, "have me assassinated if you like, but I shall not leave Madrid till its suits me to do so."

I put a commonplace seal on my letter, and had the address written by Philippe, whose hand was unknown to Manucci, and then I sent it to Pando where the king had gone.

I kept my room the whole day; and Donna Ignazia, seeing that I had recovered my spirits to some degree, made no more enquiries about the cause of my distress. I waited in the whole of the next day, expecting a reply, but in vain.

The third day, being Sunday, I went out to call on the Prince della Catolica. My carriage stopped at his door, but the porter came out and told me in a polite whisper that his highness had his reasons for not receiving me any longer.

This was an unexpected blow, but after it I was prepared for anything.

I drove to the Abbe Bigliardi, but the lackey, after taking in my name, informed me that his master was out.

I got into my carriage and went to Varnier, who said he wanted to speak to me.

"Come into my carriage," said I, "we will go and hear mass together."

On our way he told me that the Venetian ambassador, Mocenigo, had warned the Duke of Medina Sidonia that I was a dangerous character.

"The duke," he added, "replied that he would cease to know you as soon as he found out the badness of your character himself."

These three shocks, following in such quick succession, cast me into a state of confusion. I said nothing till we heard mass together, but I believe that if I had not then told him the whole story I should have had an apoplectic fit.

Varnier pitied me, and said,—

"Such are the ways of the great when they have abjured all virtue and honesty. Nevertheless, I advise you to keep silence about it, unless you would irritate Manucci still farther."

When I got home I wrote to Manucci begging him to suspend his vengeance, or else I should be obliged to tell the story to all those who insulted me for the ambassador's sake. I sent the letter to M. Soderini, the secretary of the embassy, feeling sure that he would forward it to Manucci.

I dined with my mistress, and took her to the bull fight, where I chanced to find myself in a box adjoining that in which Manucci and the two ambassadors were seated. I made them a bow which they were obliged to return, and did not vouchsafe them another glance for the rest of the spectacle.

The next day the Marquis Grimaldi refused to receive me, and I saw that I should have to abandon all hope. The Duke of Lossada remained my friend on account of his dislike to the ambassador and his unnatural tastes; but he told me that he had been requested not to receive me, and that he did not think I had the slightest chance of obtaining any employment at Court.

I could scarcely believe in such an extremity of vengeance: Manucci was making a parade of the influence he possessed over his wife the ambassador. In his insane desire for revenge he had laid all shame aside.

I was curious to know whether he had forgotten Don Emmanuel de Roda and the Marquis de la Moras; I found both of them had been forewarned against me. There was still the Count of Aranda, and I was just going to see him when a servant of his highness's came and told me that his master wished to see me.

I shuddered, for in my then state of mind I drew the most sinister conclusions from the message.

I found the great man alone, looking perfectly calm. This made me pluck up a heart. He asked me to sit down—a favour he had not hitherto done me, and this further contributed to cheer me.

"What have you been doing to offend your ambassador?" he began.

"My lord, I have done nothing to him directly, but by an inexcusable act of stupidity I have wounded his dear friend Manucci in his tenderest part. With the most innocent intentions I reposed my confidence in a cowardly fellow, who sold it to Manucci for a hundred pistoles. In his irritation, Manucci has stirred up the great man against me: 'hinc illae lacrimae'."

"You have been unwise, but what is done is done. I am sorry for you, because there is an end to all your hopes of advancement. The first thing the king would do would be to make enquiries about you of the ambassador."

"I feel it to my sorrow, my lord, but must I leave Madrid?"

"No. The ambassador did his best to make me send you way, but I told him that I had no power over you so long as you did not infringe the laws."

"'He has calumniated a Venetian subject whom I am bound to protect,' said he.

"'In that case,' I replied, 'you can resort to the ordinary law, and punish him to the best of your ability.'"

"The ambassador finally begged me to order you not to mention the matter to any Venetian subjects at Madrid, and I think you can safely promise me this."

"My lord, I have much pleasure in giving your excellency my word of honour not to do so."

"Very good. Then you can stay at Madrid as long as you please; and, indeed, Mocenigo will be leaving in the course of a week."

From that moment I made up my mind to amuse myself without any thought of obtaining a position in Spain. However, the ties of friendship made me keep up my acquaintance with Varnier, the Duke of Medina Sidonia, and the architect, Sabatini, who always gave me a warm welcome, as did his wife.

Donna Ignazia had more of my company than ever, and congratulated me on my freedom from the cares of business.

After the departure of Mocenigo I thought I would go and see if Querini, his nephew, was equally prejudiced against me. The porter told me that he had received orders not to admit me, and I laughed in the man's face.

Six or seven weeks after Manucci's departure I, too, left Madrid. I did so on compulsion, in spite of my love for Ignazia, for I had no longer hopes of doing anything in Portugal, and my purse was nearly exhausted.

I thought of selling a handsome repeater and a gold snuff-box so as to enable me to go to Marseilles, whence I thought of going to Constantinople and trying my fortune there without turning renegade. Doubtless, I should have found the plan unsuccessful, for I was attaining an age when Fortune flies. I had no reason, however, to complain of Fortune, for she had been lavish in her gifts to me, and I in my turn had always abused them.

In my state of distress the learned Abbe Pinzi introduced me to a Genoese bookseller, named Carrado, a thoroughly honest man, who seemed to have been created that the knavery of most of the Genoese might be pardoned. To him I brought my watch and snuff-box, but the worthy Carrado not only refused to buy them, but would not take them in pledge. He gave me seventeen hundred francs with no other security than my word that I would repay him if I were ever able to do so. Unhappily I have never been able to repay this debt, unless my gratitude be accounted repayment.

As nothing is sweeter than the companionship between a man and the woman he adores, so nothing is bitterer than the separation; the pleasure has vanished away, and only the pain remains.

I spent my last days at Madrid drinking the cup of pleasure which was embittered by the thought of the pain that was to follow. The worthy Diego was sad at the thought of losing me, and could with difficulty refrain from tears.

For some time my man Philippe continued to give me news of Donna Ignazia. She became the bride of a rich shoemaker, though her father was extremely mortified by her making a marriage so much beneath her station.

I had promised the Marquis de las Moras and Colonel Royas that I would come and see them at Saragossa, the capital of Aragon, and I arrived there at the beginning of September. My stay lasted for a fortnight, during which time I was able to examine the manners and customs of the Aragonese, who were not subject to the ordinances of the Marquis of Aranda, as long cloaks and low hats were to be seen at every corner. They looked like dark phantoms more than men, for the cloak covered up at least half the face. Underneath the cloak was carried el Spadino, a sword of enormous length. Persons who wore this costume were treated with great respect, though they were mostly arrant rogues; still they might possibly be powerful noblemen in disguise.

The visitor to Saragossa should see the devotion which is paid to our Lady del Pilar. I have seen processions going along the streets in which wooden statues of gigantic proportions were carried. I was taken to the best assemblies, where the monks swarmed. I was introduced to a lady of monstrous size, who, I was informed, was cousin to the famous Palafox, and I did not feel my bosom swell with pride as was evidently expected. I also made the acquaintance of Canon Pignatelli, a man of Italian origin. He was President of the Inquisition, and every morning he imprisoned the procuress who had furnished him with the girl with whom he had supped and slept. He would wake up in the morning tired out with the pleasures of the night; the girl would be driven away and the procuress imprisoned. He then dressed, confessed, said mass, and after an excellent breakfast with plenty of good wine he would send out for another girl, and this would go on day after day. Nevertheless, he was held in great respect at Saragossa, for he was a monk, a canon, and an Inquisitor.

The bull fights were finer at Saragossa than at Madrid—that is to say, they were deadlier; and the chief interest of this barbarous spectacle lies in the shedding of blood. The Marquis de las Moras and Colonel Royas gave me some excellent dinners. The marquis was one of the pleasantest men I met in Spain; he died very young two years after.

The Church of Nuestra Senora del Pilar is situated on the ramparts of the town, and the Aragonese fondly believe this portion of the town defences to be impregnable.

I had promised Donna Pelliccia to go and see her at Valentia, and on my way I saw the ancient town of Saguntum on a hill at some little distance. There was a priest travelling with me and I told him and the driver (who preferred his mules to all the antiquities in the world) that I should like to go and see the town. How the muleteer and the priest objected to this proposal!

"There are only ruins there, senor."

"That's just what I want to see."

"We shall never get to Valentia to-night."

"Here's a crown; we shall get there to-morrow."

The crown settled everything, and the man exclaimed,

"Valga me Dios, es un hombre de buen!" (So help me God, this is an honest man!) A subject of his Catholic majesty knows no heartier praise than this.

I saw the massive walls still standing and in good condition, and yet they were built during the second Punic War. I saw on two of the gateways inscriptions which to me were meaningless, but which Seguier, the old friend of the Marquis Maffei, could no doubt have deciphered.

The sight of this monument to the courage of an ancient race, who preferred to perish in the flames rather than surrender, excited my awe and admiration. The priest laughed at me, and I am sure he would not have purchased this venerable city of the dead if he could have done so by saying a mass. The very name has perished; instead of Saguntum it is called Murviedro from the Latin 'muri veteres' (old walls); but Time that destroys marble and brass destroys also the very memory of what has been.

"This place," said the priest, "is always called Murviedro."

"It is ridiculous to do so," I replied; "common sense forbids us calling a thing old which was once young enough. That's as if you would tell me that New Castille is really new."

"Well, Old Castille is more ancient than New Castille."

"No so. New Castille was only called so because it was the latest conquest; but as a matter of fact it is the older of the two."

The poor priest took refuge in silence; shaking his head, and evidently taking me for a madman.

I tried vainly to find Hannibal's head, and the inscription in honour of Caesar Claudius, but I found out the remains of the amphitheatre.

The next day I remarked the mosaic pavement, which had been discovered twenty years before.

I reached Valentia at nine o'clock in the morning, and found that I should have to content myself with a bad lodging, as Marescalchi, the opera manager, had taken all the best rooms for the members of his company. Marescalchi was accompanied by his brother, a priest, whom I found decidedly learned for his age. We took a walk together, and he laughed when I proposed going into a cafe, for there was not such a thing in the town. There were only taverns of the lowest class where the wine is not fit to drink. I could scarcely believe it, but Spain is a peculiar country. When I was at Valentia, a good bottle of wine was scarcely obtainable, though Malaga and Alicante were both close at hand.

In the first three days of my stay at Valentia (the birthplace of Alexander VI.), I saw all the objects of interest in the town, and was confirmed in my idea that what seems so admirable in the descriptions of writers and the pictures of artists loses much of its charm on actual inspection.

Though Valentia is blessed with an excellent climate, though it is well watered, situated in the midst of a beautiful country, fertile in all the choicest products of nature, though it is the residence of many of the most distinguished of the Spanish nobility, though its women are the most handsome in Spain, though it has the advantage of being the seat of an archbishop; in spite of all these commodities, it is a most disagreeable town to live in. One is ill lodged and ill fed, there is no good wine and no good company, there is not even any intellectual provision, for though there is a university, lettered men are absolutely unknown.

As for the bridges, churches, the arsenal, the exchange, the town hall, the twelve town gates, and the rest, I could not take pleasure in a town where the streets are not paved, and where a public promenade is conspicuous by its absence. Outside the town the country is delightful, especially on the side towards the sea; but the outside is not the inside.

The feature which pleased me most was the number of small one-horse vehicles which transport the traveller rapidly from one point to another, at a very slight expense, and will even undertake a two or three days' journey.

If my frame of mind had been a more pleasant one, I should have travelled through the kingdoms of Murcia and Grenada, which surpass Italy in beauty and fertility.

Poor Spaniards! This beauty and fertility of your land are the cause of your ignorance, as the mines of Peru and Potosi have brought about that foolish pride and all the prejudices which degrade you.

Spaniards, when will the impulse come? when will you shake off that fatal lethargy? Now you are truly useless to yourselves, and the rest of the world; what is it you need?

A furious revolution, a terrible shock, a conquest of regeneration; your case is past gentle methods, it needs the cautery and the fire.

The first call I paid was on Donna Pelliccia. The first performance was to be given in two days. This was not a matter of any difficulty, as the same operas were to be presented as had been already played at Aranjuez, the Escurial, and the Granja, for the Count of Aranda would never have dared to sanction the performance of an Italian comic opera at Madrid. The novelty would have been too great, and the Inquisition would have interfered.

The balls were a considerable shock, and two years after they were suppressed. Spain will never make any real advance, until the Inquisition is suppressed also.

As soon as Donna Pelliccia arrived, she sent in the letter of introduction she had received from the Duke of Arcos, three months before. She had not seen the duke since their meeting at Aranjuez.

"Madam," said Don Diego, the person to whom she was commended, "I have come to offer you my services, and to tell you of the orders his grace has laid on me, of which you may possibly be ignorant."

"I hope, sir," she replied, "that I am not putting you to any inconvenience, but I am extremely grateful to the duke and to yourself; and I shall have the honour of calling on you to give you my thanks."

"Not at all; I have only to say that I have orders to furnish you with any sums you may require, to the amount of twenty-five thousand doubloons."

"Twenty-five thousand doubloons?"

"Exactly, madam, two hundred and fifty thousand francs in French money, and no more. Kindly read his grace's letter; you do not seem to be aware of its contents."

The letter was a brief one:

"Don Diego,—You will furnish Donna Pelliccia with whatever sums she may require, not exceeding twenty-five thousand doubloons, at my account. "THE DUKE DOS ARCOS"

We remained in a state of perfect stupefaction. Donna Pelliccia returned the epistle to the banker, who bowed and took his leave.

This sounds almost incredible generosity, but in Spain such things are not uncommon. I have already mentioned the munificent gift of Medina-Celi to Madame Pichona.

Those who are unacquainted with the peculiar Spanish character and the vast riches of some of the nobility, may pronounce such acts of generosity to be ridiculous and positively injurious, but they make a mistake. The spendthrift gives and squanders by a kind of instinct, and so he will continue to do as long as his means remain. But these splendid gifts I have described do not come under the category of senseless prodigality. The Spaniard is chiefly ambitious of praise, for praise he will do anything; but this very desire for admiration serves to restrain him from actions by which he would incur blame. He wants to be thought superior to his fellows, as the Spanish nation is superior to all other nations; he wants to be thought worthy of a throne, and to be considered as the possessor of all the virtues.

I may also note that while some of the Spanish nobility are as rich as the English lords, the former have not so many ways of spending their money as the latter, and thus are enabled to be heroically generous on occasion.

As soon as Don Diego had gone, we began to discuss the duke's noble behaviour.

Donna Pelliccia maintained that the duke had wished to shew his confidence in her by doing her the honour of supposing her incapable of abusing his generosity; "at all events," she concluded, "I would rather die of hunger than take a single doubloon of Don Diego."

"The duke would be offended," said a violinist; "I think you ought to take something."

"You must take it all," said the husband.

I was of the lady's opinion, and told her that I was sure the duke would reward her delicacy by making her fortune.

She followed my advice and her own impulse, though the banker remonstrated with her.

Such is the perversity of the human mind that no one believed in Donna Pelliccia's delicacy. When the king heard what had happened he ordered the worthy actress to leave Madrid, to prevent the duke ruining himself.

Such is often the reward of virtue here below, but the malicious persons who had tried to injure Donna Pelliccia by calumniating her to the king were the means of making her fortune.

The duke who had only spoken once or twice to the actress in public, and had never spent a penny on her, took the king's command as an insult, and one not to be borne. He was too proud to solicit the king to revoke the order he had given, and in the end behaved in a way befitting so noble-minded a man. For the first time he visited Donna Pelliccia at her own house, and begging her to forgive him for having been the innocent cause of her disgrace, asked her to accept a rouleau and a letter which he laid on the table.

The rouleau contained a hundred gold ounces with the words "for travelling expenses," and the letter was addressed to a Roman bank, and proved to be an order for twenty-four thousand Roman crowns.

For twenty-nine years this worthy woman kept an establishment at Rome, and did so in a manner which proved her worthy of her good fortune.

The day after Donna Pelliccia's departure the king saw the Duke of Arcos, and told him not to be sad, but to forget the woman, who had been sent away for his own good.

"By sending her away, your majesty obliged me to turn fiction into fact, for I only knew her by speaking to her in various public places, and I had never made her the smallest present."

"Then you never gave her twenty-five thousand doubloons?"

"Sire, I gave her double that sum, but only on the day before yesterday. Your majesty has absolute power, but if she had not received her dismissal I should never have gone to her house, nor should I have given her the smallest present."

The king was stupefied and silent; he was probably meditating on the amount of credit a monarch should give to the gossip that his courtiers bring him.

I heard about this from M. Monnino, who was afterwards known under the title of Castille de Florida Blanca, and is now living in exile in Murcia, his native country.

After Marescalchi had gone, and I was making my preparations for my journey to Barcelona, I saw one day, at the bull fight, a woman whose appearance had a strange kind of fascination about it.

There was a knight of Alcantara at my side, and I asked him who the lady was.

"She is the famous Nina."

"How famous?"

"If you do not know her story, it is too long to be told here."

I could not help gazing at her, and two minutes later an ill-looking fellow beside her came up to my companion and whispered something in his ear.

The knight turned towards me and informed me in the most polite manner that the lady whose name I had asked desired to know mine.

I was silly enough to be flattered by her curiosity, and told the messenger that if the lady would allow me I would come to her box and tell her my name in person after the performance.

"From your accent I should suppose you were an Italian."

"I am a Venetian."

"So is she."

When he had gone away my neighbour seemed inclined to be more communicative, and informed me that Nina was a dancer whom the Count de Ricla, the Viceroy of Barcelona, was keeping for some weeks at Valentia, till he could get her back to Barcelona, whence the bishop of the diocese had expelled her on account of the scandals to which she gave rise. "The count," he added, "is madly in love with her, and allows her fifty doubloons a day."

"I should hope she does not spend them."

"She can't do that, but she does not let a day pass without committing some expensive act of folly."

I felt curious to know a woman of such a peculiar character, and longed for the end of the bull fight, little thinking in what trouble this new acquaintance would involve me.

She received me with great politeness, and as she got into her carriage drawn by six mules, she said she would be delighted if I would breakfast with her at nine o'clock on the following day.

I promised to come, and I kept my word.

Her house was just outside the town walls, and was a very large building. It was richly and tastefully furnished, and was surrounded by an enormous garden.

The first thing that struck me was the number of the lackeys and the richness of their liveries, and the maids in elegant attire, who seemed to be going and coming in all directions.

As I advanced I heard an imperious voice scolding some one.

The scold was Nina, who was abusing an astonished-looking man, who was standing by a large table covered with stuffs and laces.

"Excuse me," said she, "but this fool of a Spaniard wants to persuade me that this lace is really handsome."

She asked me what I thought of the lace, and though I privately thought it lace of the finest quality, I did not care to contradict her, and so replied that I was no judge.

"Madam," said the tradesman, "if you do not like the lace, leave it; will you keep the stuffs?"

"Yes," she replied; "and as for the lace, I will shew you that it is not the money that deters me."

So saying the mad girl took up a pair of scissors and cut the lace into fragments.

"What a pity!" said the man who had spoken to me at the bull fight.
"People will say that you have gone off your head."

"Be silent, you pimping rogue!" said she, enforcing her words with a sturdy box on the ear.

The fellow went off, calling her strumpet, which only made her scream with laughter; then, turning to the Spaniard, she told him to make out his account directly.

The man did not want telling twice, and avenged himself for the abuse he had received by the inordinate length of his bill.

She took up the account and placed her initials at the bottom without deigning to look at the items, and said,—

"Go to Don Diego Valencia; he will pay you immediately."

As soon as we were alone the chocolate was served, and she sent a message to the fellow whose ears she had boxed to come to breakfast directly.

"You needn't be surprised at my way of treating him," she said. "He's a rascal whom Ricla has placed in my house to spy out my actions, and I treat him as you have seen, so that he may have plenty of news to write to his master."

I thought I must be dreaming; such a woman seemed to me beyond the limits of the possible.

The poor wretch, who came from Bologna and was a musician by profession, came and sat down with us without a word. His name was Molinari.

As soon as he had finished his breakfast he left the room, and Nina spent an hour with me talking about Spain, Italy, and Portugal, where she had married a dancer named Bergonzi.

"My father," she said, "was the famous charlatan Pelandi; you may have known him at Venice."

After this piece of confidence (and she did not seem at all ashamed of her parentage) she asked me to sup with her, supper being her favourite meal. I promised to come, and I left her to reflect on the extraordinary character of the woman, and on the good fortune which she so abused.

Nina was wonderfully beautiful; but as it has always been my opinion that mere beauty does not go for much, I could not understand how a viceroy could have fallen in love with her to such an extent. As for Molinari, after which I had seen, I could only set him down as an infamous wretch.

I went to supper with her for amusement's sake, for, with all her beauty, she had not touched my heart in the slightest degree. It was at the beginning of October, but at Valentia the thermometer marked twenty degrees Reaumur in the shade.

Nina was walking in the garden with her companion, both of them being very lightly clad; indeed, Nina had only her chemise and a light petticoat.

As soon as she saw me she came up and begged me to follow their example in the way of attire, but I begged to be excused. The presence of that hateful fellow revolted me in the highest degree.

In the interval before supper Nina entertained me with a number of lascivious anecdotes of her experiences from the time she began her present mode of living up to the age of twenty-two, which was her age then.

If it had not been for the presence of the disgusting Argus, no doubt all these stories would have produced their natural effect on me; but as it was they had none whatever.

We had a delicate supper and ate with appetite, and after it was over I would have gladly left them; but Nina would not let me go. The wine had taken effect, and she wished to have a little amusement.

After all the servants had been dismissed, this Messalina ordered Molinari to strip naked, and she then began to treat him in a manner which I cannot describe without disgust.

The rascal was young and strong, and, though he was drunk, Nina's treatment soon placed him in a hearty condition. I could see that she wished me to play my part in the revels, but my disgust had utterly deprived me of all my amorous faculties.

Nina, too, had undressed, and seeing that I viewed the orgy coldly she proceeded to satiate her desires by means of Molinari.

I had to bear with the sight of this beautiful woman coupling herself with an animal, whose only merit lay in his virile monstrosity, which she no doubt regarded as a beauty.

When she had exhausted her amorous fury she threw herself into a bath, then came back, drank a bottle of Malmsey Madeira, and finally made her brutal lover drink till he fell on to the floor.

I fled into the next room, not being able to bear it any longer, but she followed me. She was still naked, and seating herself beside me on an ottoman she asked me how I had enjoyed the spectacle.

I told her boldy that the disgust with which her wretched companion had inspired me was so great that it had utterly annulled the effect of her charms.

"That may be so, but now he is not here, and yet you do nothing. One would not think it, to look at you."

"You are right, for I have my feelings like any other man, but he has disgusted me too much. Wait till tomorrow, and let me not see that monster so unworthy of enjoying you."

"He does not enjoy me. If I thought he did I would rather die than let him have to do with me, for I detest him."

"What! you do not love him, and yet you make use of him in the way you do?"

"Yes, just as I might use a mechanical instrument."

In this woman I saw an instance of the depths of degradation to which human nature may be brought.

She asked me to sup with her on the following day, telling me that we would be alone, as Molinari would be ill.

"He will have got over the effects of the wine."

"I tell you he will be ill. Come to-morrow, and come every evening."

"I am going the day after to-morrow."

"You will not go for a week, and then we will go together."

"That's impossible."

"If you go you will insult me beyond bearing."

I went home with my mind made up to depart without having anything more to do with her; and though I was far from inexperienced in wickedness of all kinds, I could not help feeling astonished at the unblushing frankness of this Megaera, who had told me what I already knew, but in words that I had never heard a woman use before.

"I only use him to satisfy my desires, and because I am certain that he does not love me; if I thought he did I would rather die than allow him to do anything with me, for I detest him."

The next day I went to her at seven o'clock in the evening. She received me with an air of feigned melancholy, saying,—

"Alas! we shall have to sup alone; Molinari has got the colic."

"You said he would be ill; have you poisoned him?"

"I am quite capable of doing so, but I hope I never shall."

"But you have given him something?"

"Only what he likes himself; but we will talk of that again. Let us sup and play till to-morrow, and tomorrow evening we will begin again."

"I am going away at seven o'clock to-morrow."

"No, no, you are not; and your coachman will have no cause for complaint, for he has been paid; here is the receipt."

These remarks, delivered with an air of amorous despotism, flattered my vanity. I made up my mind to submit gaily, called her wanton, and said I was not worth the pains she was taking over me.

"What astonishes me," said I, "is that with this fine house you do not care to entertain company."

"Everybody is afraid to come; they fear Ricla's jealousy, for it is well known that that animal who is now suffering from the colic tells him everything I do. He swears that it is not so, but I know him to be a liar. Indeed, I am very glad he does write to Ricla, and only wish he had something of real importance to write about."

"He will tell him that I have supped alone with you."

"All the better; are you afraid?"

"No; but I think you ought to tell me if I have anything really to fear."

"Nothing at all; it will fall on me."

"But I should not like to involve you in a dispute which might be prejudicial to your interests."

"Not at all; the more I provoke him, the better he loves me, and I will make him pay dearly when he asks me to make it up."

"Then you don't love him?"

"Yes, to ruin him; but he is so rich that there doesn't seem much hope of my ever doing that."

Before me I saw a woman as beautiful as Venus and as degraded as Lucifer; a woman most surely born to be the ruin of anyone who had the misfortune to fall in love with her. I had known women of similar character, but never one so dangerous as she.

I determined to make some money out of her if I could.

She called for cards, and asked me to play with her at a game called primiera. It is a game of chance, but of so complicated a nature that the best player always wins. In a quarter of an hour I found that I was the better player, but she had such luck that at the end of the game I had lost twenty pistoles, which I paid on the spot. She took the money, promising to give me my revenge.

We had supper, and then we committed all the wantonness she wished and I was capable of performing, for with me the age of miracles was past.

The next day I called to see her earlier in the evening. We played again; and she lost, and went on losing evening after evening, till I had won a matter of two or three hundred doubloons, no unwelcome addition to my somewhat depleted purse.

The spy recovered from his colic and supped with us every evening, but his presence no longer interfered with my pleasure since Nina had ceased to prostitute herself to him in my presence. She did the opposite; giving herself to me, and telling him to write to the Comte de Ricla whatever he liked.

The count wrote her a letter which she gave me to read. The poor love-sick viceroy informed her that she might safely return to Barcelona, as the bishop had received an order from the Court to regard her as merely au actress, whose stay in his diocese would only be temporary; she would thus be allowed to live there in peace so long as she abstained from giving cause for scandal. She told me that whilst she was at Barcelona I could only see her after ten o'clock at night, when the count always left her. She assured me that I should run no risk whatever.

Possibly I should not have stayed at Barcelona at all if Nina had not told me that she would always be ready to lend me as much money as I wanted.

She asked me to leave Valentia a day before her, and to await her at Tarragona. I did so, and spent a very pleasant day in that town, which abounds in remains of antiquity.

I ordered a choice supper according to her instructions, and took care that she should have a separate bedroom so as to avoid any scandal.

She started in the morning begging me to wait till the evening, and to travel by night so as to reach Barcelona by day-time. She told me to put up at the "Santa Maria," and not to call till I had heard from her.

I followed all the directions given me by this curious woman, and found myself comfortably lodged at Barcelona. My landlord was a Swiss who told me in confidence that he had received instructions to treat me well, and that I had only to ask for what I wanted.

We shall see soon what was the result of all this.

CHAPTER VIII

My Imprudence—Passano—I Am Imprisoned—My Departure from Barcelona—Madame Castelbajac at Montpellier—Nîmes—I Arrive at Aix

Although my Swiss landlord seemed an honest and trustworthy kind of man, I could not help thinking that Nina had acted very imprudently in commending me to him. She was the viceroy's mistress; and though the viceroy might be a very agreeable man, he was a Spaniard, and not likely to be easy-going in his love affairs. Nina herself had told me that he was ardent, jealous, and suspicious. But the mischief was done, and there was no help for it.

When I got up my landlord brought me a valet de place, for whose character he said he could answer, and he then sent up an excellent dinner. I had slept till three o'clock in the afternoon.

After dinner I summoned my host, and asked him whether Nina had told him to get me a servant. He answered in the affirmative, and added that a carriage was awaiting my commands at the door; it had been taken by the week.

"I am astonished to hear it, for no one but myself can say what I can afford or not."

"Sir, everything is paid for."

"Paid for! I will not have it!"

"You can settle that with her, but I shall certainly take no payment."

I saw dangers ahead, but as I have never cared to cherish forbodings I dismissed the idea.

I had a letter of introduction from the Marquis de las Moras to Don Miguel de Cevallos, and another from Colonel Royas to Don Diego de la Secada. I took my letters, and the next day Don Diego came to see me, and took me to the Comte de Peralda. The day after Don Miguel introduced me to the Comte de Ricla, Viceroy of Catalonia, and the lover of Nina.

The Comte de Peralada was a young man with a pleasant face but with an ill-proportioned body. He was a great debauchee and lover of bad company, an enemy of religion, morality, and law. He was directly descended from the Comte de Peralada, who served Philip II. so well that this king declared him "count by the grace of God." The original patent of nobility was the first thing I saw in his antechamber, where it was framed and glazed so that all visitors might see it in the quarter of an hour they were kept waiting.

The count received me with an easy and cordiale manner, which seemed to say that he renounced all the dignities of his rank. He thanked Don Diego for introducing me, and talked a good deal about Colonel Royas. He asked me if I had seen the English girl he was keeping at Saragossa, and on my replying in the affirmative, he told me in a whisper that he had slept with her.

He took me to his stables, where he had some splendid horses, and then asked me to dine with him the next day.

The viceroy received me in a very different manner; he stood up so that he might not have to offer me a chair, and though I spoke

Italian, with which language I knew him to be well acquainted, he answered me in Spanish, styling me 'ussia' (a contraction of 'vuestra senoria', your lordship, and used by everyone in Spain), while I gave him his proper title of excellence.

He talked a good deal about Madrid, and complained that M. de Mocenigo had gone to Paris by Bayonne instead of Barcelona, as he had promised him.

I tried to excuse my ambassador by saying that by taking the other route he had saved fifty leagues of his journey, but the viceroy replied that 'tenir la palabra' (keeping to one's words) comes before all else.

He asked me if I thought of staying long at Barcelona, and seemed surprised when I told him that, with his leave, I hoped to make a long stay.

"I hope you will enjoy yourself," he said, "but I must warn you that if you indulge in the pleasures which my nephew Peralada will doubtless offer you, you will not enjoy a very good reputation at Barcelona."

As the Comte de Ricla made this observation in public, I thought myself justified in communicating it to Peralada himself. He was delighted, and told me, with evident vanity, that he had gone to Madrid three times, and had been ordered to return to Catalonia on each occasion.

I thought my best plan would be to follow the viceroy's indirect advice, so I refused to join in any of the little parties of pleasure which Peralada proposed.

On the fifth day after my arrival, an officer came to ask me to dinner at the viceroy's. I accepted the invitation with much pleasure, for I had been afraid of the viceroy's having heard of my relations with Nina, and thought it possible that he might have taken a dislike to me. He was very pleasant to me at dinner, often addressing his observations to me, but always in a tone of great gravity.

I had been in Barcelona for a week, and was beginning to wonder why I had not heard from Nina; but one evening she wrote me a note, begging me to come on foot and alone to her house at ten o'clock the same night.

If I had been wise I should not have gone, for I was not in love with the woman, and should have remembered the respect due to the viceroy; but I was devoid of all wisdom and prudence. All the misfortunes I have experienced in my long life never taught me those two most necessary virtues.

At the hour she had named I called on her, wearing my great coat, and with a sword for my only weapon. I found Nina with her sister, a woman of thirty-six or thereabouts, who was married to an Italian dancer, nicknamed Schizza, because he had a flatter nose than any Tartar.

Nina had just been supping with her lover, who had left her at ten o'clock, according to his invariable custom.

She said she was delighted to hear I had been to dinner with him, as she had herself spoken to him in my praise, saying how admirably I had kept her company at Valentia.

"I am glad to hear it, but I do not think you are wise in inviting me to your house at such late hours."

"I only do so to avoid scandal amongst my neighbours."

"In my opinion my coming so late is only likely to increase the probability of scandal, and to make your viceroy jealous."

"He will never hear of your coming."

"I think you are mistaken."

I went away at midnight, after a conversation of the most decent character. Her sister did not leave us for a moment, and Nina gave her no cause to suspect the intimacy of our relations.

I went to see her every evening, without encroaching on the count's preserves. I thought myself secure, but the following warning should have made me desist if I had not been carried away by the forces of destiny and obstinacy in combination.

An officer in the Walloon Guards accosted me one day as I was walking by myself just outside the town. He begged me in the most polite manner to excuse him if he spoke on a matter which was indifferent to him but of great consequence to me.

"Speak, sir," I replied, "I will take whatever you say in good part."

"Very good. You are a stranger, sir, and may not be acquainted with our Spanish manners, consequently you are unaware of the great risk you run in going to see Nina every evening after the count has left her."

"What risk do I run? I have no doubt that the count knows all about it and does not object."

"I have no doubt as to his knowing it, and he may possibly pretend to know nothing before her, as he fears as well as loves her; but if she tells you that he does not object, she either deceives herself or you. He cannot love her without being jealous, and a jealous Spaniard . . .

"Follow my advice, sir, and forgive my freedom."

"I am sincerely obliged to you for your kind interest in me, but I cannot follow your advice, as by doing so I should be wanting in politeness to Nina, who likes to see me and gives me a warm welcome. I shall continue to visit her till she orders me not to do so, or till the count signifies to me his displeasure at my visits to his mistress."

"The count will never do such a thing; he is too careful of his dignity."

The worthy officer then narrated to me all the acts of injustice which Ricla had committed since he had fallen in love with this woman. He had dismissed gentlemen from his service on the mere suspicion that they were in love with her; some had been exiled, and others imprisoned on one frivolous pretext or another. Before he had known Nina he had been a pattern of wisdom, justice, and virtue, and now he had become unjust, cruel, blindly passionate, and in every way a scandal to the high position he occupied.

All this should have influenced me, but it had not the slightest effect. I told him for politeness' sake that I would endeavour to part from her by degrees, but I had no intention of doing so.

When I asked him how he knew that I visited Nina, he laughed and said it was a common topic of conversation all over the town.

The same evening I called on her without mentioning my conversation with the officer. There would have been some excuse for me if I had been in love with her, but as it was . . . I acted like a madman.

On the 14th of November I went to see her at the usual time. I found her with a man who was shewing her miniatures. I looked at him and found that he was the scoundrel Passano, or Pogomas.

My blood boiled; I took Nina's hand and led her into a neighbouring room, and told her to dismiss the rogue at once, or I would go to return no more.

"He's a painter."

"I am well acquainted with his history, and will tell you all about it presently; but send him away, or I shall go."

She called her sister, and told her to order the Genoese to leave the house and never to enter it again.

The thing was 'done in a moment, but the sister told us that as he went out he had said,—

"Se ne pentira." ("He shall be sorry for it.").

I occupied an hour in relating some of the injuries I had received from this scoundrelly fellow.

The next day (November 15th), I went to Nina at the usual time, and after spending two hours in pleasant converse with her and her sister I went out as the clocks were striking midnight.

The door of the house was under an arcade, which extended to the end of the street. It was a dark night; and I had scarcely gone twenty-five paces when two men suddenly rushed at me.

I stepped back, drawing my sword, and exclaiming, "Assassins!" and then with a rapid movement, I thrust my blade into the body of the nearest assailant. I then left the arcade, and began to run down the street. The second assassin fired a pistol at me, but it fortunately missed me. I fell down and dropped my hat in my rapid flight, and got up and continued my course without troubling to pick it up. I did not know whether I was wounded or not, but at last I got to my inn, and laid down the bloody sword on the counter, under the landlord's nose. I was quite out of breath.

I told the landlord what had happened, and on taking off my great coat, I found it to be pierced in two places just below the armpit.

"I am going to bed," I said to the landlord, "and I leave my great coat and the sword in your charge. Tomorrow morning I shall ask you to come with me before the magistrate to denounce this act of assassination, for if the man was killed it must be shewn that I only slew him to save my own life."

"I think your best plan would be to fly Barcelona immediately."

"Then you think I have not told you the strict truth?"

"I am sure you have; but I know whence the blow comes, and God knows what will befall you!"

"Nothing at all; but if I fly I shall be accounted guilty. Take care of the sword; they tried to assassinate me, but I think the assassins got the worst of it."

I went to bed somewhat perturbed, but I had the consoling thought that if I had killed a man I had done so to self-defence; my conscience was quite clear.

At seven o'clock the next morning I heard a knocking at my door. I opened it, and saw my landlord, accompanied by an officer, who told me to give him all my papers, to dress, and to follow him, adding that he should be compelled to use force in case of resistance.

"I have no intention of resisting," I replied. "By whose authority do you ask me for my papers?"

"By the authority of the governor. They will be returned to you if nothing suspicious is found amongst them."

"Where are you going to take me?"

"To the citadel."

I opened my trunk, took out my linen and my clothes, which I gave to my landlord, and I saw the officer's astonishment at seeing my trunk half filled with papers.

"These are all the papers I have," I said. I locked the box and gave the officer the key.

"I advise you, sir," he said, "to put all necessary articles into a portmanteau." He then ordered the landlord to send me a bed, and finally asked me if I had any papers in my pockets.

"Only my passports."

"That's exactly what we want," he rejoined, with a grim smile.

"My passports are sacred; I will never give them to anyone but the governor-general. Reverence your king; here is his passport, here is that of the Count of Aranda, and here the passport of the Venetian ambassador. You will have to bind me hand and foot before you get them."

"Be more moderate, sir. In giving them to me it is just as if you gave them to the viceroy. If you resist I will not bind you hand and foot, but I shall take you before the viceroy, and then you will be forced to give them up in public. Give them to me with a good grace, and you shall have an acknowledgement."

The worthy landlord told me I should be wiser to give in, so I let myself be persuaded. The officer gave me a full quittance, which I put in my pocketbook (this he let me keep out of his kindness), and then I followed him. He had six constables with him, but they kept a good distance away. Comparing this with the circumstances of my arrest at Madrid, I thought myself well treated.

Before we left the inn the officer told me that I might order what meals I pleased, and I asked the landlord to let me have my dinner and supper as usual.

On the way I told him of my adventure of the night before; he listened attentively but made no comments.

When we reached the citadel I was delivered to the officer of the guard, who gave me a room on the first floor. It was bare of furniture, but the windows looked on to a square and had no iron bars.

I had scarcely been there ten minutes when my carpet bag and an excellent bed were brought in.

As soon as I was alone I began to think over the situation. I finished where I ought to have begun.

"What can this imprisonment have to do with my last night's adventure?" I reflected.

I could not make out the connection.

"They are bent on examining my papers; they must think I have been tampering in some political or religious intrigue; but my mind is quite at ease on that score. I am well lodged at present, and no doubt shall be set free after my papers have been examined; they can find nothing against me there.

"The affair of my attempted assassination will, no doubt, be considered separately.

"Even if the rascal is dead, I do not see what they can do to me.

"On the other hand, my landlord's advice to fly from Barcelona looks ominous; what if the assassins received their orders from some person high in authority?

"It is possible that Ricla may have vowed my ruin, but it does not seem probable to me.

"Would it have been wise to follow the landlord's advice?

"Possibly, but I do not think so; my honour would have suffered, and I might have been caught and laid up in some horrid dungeon, whereas for a prison I am comfortable enough here.

"In three or four days the examination of my papers will have been completed, and as there is nothing in them likely to be offensive to the powers that be, they will be returned to me with my liberty, which will taste all the sweeter for this short deprivation.

"As for my passports they all speak in my favour.

"I cannot think that the all-powerful hand of the viceroy could have directed the assassin's sword; it would be a dishonour to him, and if it were so, he would not be treating me so kindly now. If it were his doing, he must have heard directly that the blow had failed, and in that case I do not think he would have arrested me this morning.

"Shall I write to Nina? Will writing be allowed here?"

As I was puzzling my brains with these reflections, stretched on my bed (for I had no chair), I heard some disturbance, and on opening my window I saw, to my great astonishment, Passano being brought into the prison by a corporal and two soldiers. As he was going in, the rascal looked up and saw me, and began to laugh.

"Alas!" I said to myself, "here is fresh food for conjecture. The fellow told Nina's sister that I should be sorry for what I had done. He must have directed some fearful calumny against me, and they are imprisoning him so as to be sure of his evidence."

On reflection, I was well pleased at the turn affairs had taken.

An excellent dinner was set before me, but I had no chair or table. The deficiency was remedied by the soldier who was in charge of me for the consideration of a duro.

Prisoners were not allowed to have pen and ink without special permission; but paper and pencils were not included under this regulation, so my guard got them for me, together with candles and candlesticks, and I proceeded to kill time by making geometrical calculations. I made the obliging soldier sup with me, and he promised to commend me to one of his comrades who would serve me well. The guard was relieved at eleven.

On the fourth day the officer of the guard came to me with a distressed look, and told me that he had the disagreeable duty of giving me some very bad news.

"What is that, sir?"

"I have received orders to transfer you to the bottom of the tower."

"To transfer me?"

"Yes."

"Then they must have discovered in me a criminal of the deepest dye! Let us go at once."

I found myself in a kind of round cellar, paved with large flagstones, and lighted by five or six narrow slits in the walls. The officer told me I must order what food required to be brought once a day, as no one was allowed to come into the 'calabozo', or dungeon, by night.

"How about lights?"

"You may lave one lamp always burning, and that will be enough, as books are not allowed. When your dinner is brought, the officer on duty will open the pies and the poultry to see that they do not contain any documents; for here no letters are allowed to come in or go out."

"Have these orders been given for my especial benefit?"

"No, sir; it is the ordinary rule. You will be able to converse with the sentinel."

"The door will be open, then?"

"Not at all."

"How about the cleanliness of my cell?"

"A soldier will accompany the officer in charge of your dinner, and he will attend to your wants for a trifle."

"May I amuse myself by making architectural plans with the pencil?"

"As much as you like."

"Then will you be good enough to order some paper to be bought for me?"

"With pleasure."

The officer seemed to pity me as he left me, and bolted and barred the heavy door behind which I saw a man standing sentry with his bayonet fixed. The door was fitted with a small iron grating.

When I got my paper and my dinner at noonday the officer cut open a fowl, and plunged a fork in the other dishes so as to make sure that there were no papers at the bottom.

My dinner would have sufficed for six people. I told the officer that I should be much honoured by his dining with me, but he replied that it was strictly forbidden. He gave me the same answer when I asked if I might have the newspapers.

It was a festival time for the sentinels, as I shared my meals and my good wine with them; and consequently these poor fellows were firmly attached to me.

I was curious to know who was paying for my good cheer, but there was no chance of my finding out, for the waiter from the inn was never allowed to approach my cell.

In this dungeon, where I was imprisoned for forty-two days, I wrote in pencil and without other reference than my memory, my refutation of Amelot de la Houssaye's "History of the Venetian Government."

I was most heartily amused during my imprisonment, and in the following manner:

While I was at Warsaw an Italian named Tadini came to Warsaw. He had an introduction to Tomatis who commended him to me. He called himself an oculist. Tomatis used to give him a dinner now and again, but not being well off in those days I could only give him good words and a cup of coffee when he chanced to come about my breakfast-time.

Tadini talked to everybody about the operations he had performed, and condemned an oculist who had been at Warsaw for twenty years, saying that he did not understand how to extract a cataract, while the other oculist said that Tadini was a charlatan who did not know how the eye was made.

Tadini begged me to speak in his favour to a lady who had had a cataract removed by the Warsaw oculist, only to return again a short time after the operation.

The lady was blind of the one eye, but she could see with the other, and
I told Tadini that I did not care to meddle with such a delicate matter.

"I have spoken to the lady," said Tadini, "and I have mentioned your name as a person who will answer for me."

"You have done wrong; in such a matter I would not stand surety for the most learned of men, and I know nothing about your learning."

"But you know I am an oculist."

"I know you were introduced to me as such, but that's all. As a professional man, you should not need anyone's commendation, you should be able to say, 'Operibus credite'. That should be your motto."

Tadini was vexed with my incredulity, and shewed me a number of testimonials, which I might possibly have read, if the first which met my eye had not been from a lady who protested to all and singular that M. Tadini had cured her of amaurosis. At this I laughed in his face and told him to leave me alone.

A few days after I found myself dining with him at the house of the lady with the cataract. She had almost made up her mind to submit to the operation, but as the rascal had mentioned my name, she wanted me to be present at a dispute between Tadini and the other oculist who came in with the dessert.

I disposed myself to listen to the arguments of the two rival professors with considerable pleasure. The Warsaw oculist was a German, but spoke French very well; however, he attacked Tadini in Latin. The Italian checked him by saying that their discourse must be conducted in a language intelligible to the lady, and I agreed with him. It was plain that Tadini did not know a word of Latin.

The German oculist began by admitting that after the operation for cataract there was no chance of the disease returning, but that there was a considerable risk of the crystalline humour evaporating, and the patient being left in a state of total blindness.

Tadini, instead of denying this statement (which was inaccurate), had the folly to take a little box out of his pocket. It contained a number of minute round crystals.

"What's that?" said the old professor.

"A substance which I can place in the cornea to supply the loss of the crystalline matter."

The German went off into a roar of laughter so long and loud that the lady could not help laughing. I should have liked to join them, but I was ashamed to be thought the patron of this ignorant fellow, so I preserved a gloomy silence.

Tadini no doubt interpreted my silence as a mark of disapproval of the German's laughter, and thought to better matters by asking me to give my opinion.

"As you want to hear it," said I, "here it is."

"There's a great difference between a tooth and the crystalline humour; and though you may have succeeded in putting an artificial tooth into a gum, this treatment will not do with the eye."

"Sir, I am not a dentist."

"No, nor an oculist either."

At this the ignorant rascal got up and left the room, and it was decidedly the best thing he could do.

We laughed over this new treatment, and the lady promised to have nothing more to do with him. The professor was not content to despise his opponent in silence. He had him cited before the Faculty of Medicine to be examined on his knowledge of the eye, and procured the insertion of a satiric article in the news on the new operation for replacing the crystalline humour, alluding to the wonderful artist then in Warsaw who could perform this operation as easily as a dentist could put in a false tooth.

This made Tadini furious, and he set upon the old professor in the street and forced him to the refuge in a house.

After this he no doubt left the town on foot, for he was seen no more. Now the reader is in a position to understand my surprise and amusement, when, one day as I peered through the grating in my dungeon, I saw the oculist Tadini standing over me with gun in hand. But he at all events evinced no amusement whatever, while I roared and roared again with laughter for the two hours his duty lasted.

I gave him a good meal and a sufficiency of my excellent wine, and at the end a crown, promising that he should have the same treatment every time he returned to the post. But I only saw him four times, as the guard at my cell was a position eagerly coveted and intrigued for by the other soldiers.

He amused me by the story of his misadventures since he had left Warsaw. He had travelled far and wide without making a fortune, and at last arrived in Barcelona, where he failed to meet with any courtesy or consideration. He had no introduction, no diploma; he had refused to submit to an examination in the Latin tongue, because (as he said) there was no connection between the learned languages and the diseases of the eye; and the result was that, instead of the common fate of being ordered to leave the country, he was made into a soldier. He told me in confidence that he intended to desert, but he said he should take care to avoid the galleys.

"What have you done with your crystals?"

"I have renounced them since I left Warsaw, though I am sure they would succeed."

I never heard of him again.

On December 28th, six weeks after my arrest, the officer of the guard came to my cell and told me to dress and follow him.

"Where are we going?"

"I am about to deliver you to an officer of the viceroy, who is waiting."

I dressed hastily, and after placing all my belongings in a portmanteau I followed him. We went to the guardroom, and there I was placed under the charge of the officer who had arrested me, who took me to the palace. There a Government official shewed me my trunk, telling me that I should find all my papers intact; and he then returned me my three passports, with the remark that they were genuine documents.

"I knew that all along."

"I suppose so, but we had reasons for doubting their authenticity."

"They must have been strange reasons, for, as you now confess, these reasons were devoid of reason."

"You must be aware that I cannot reply to such an objection."

"I don't ask you to do so."

"Your character is perfectly clear; all the same I must request you to leave Barcelona in three days, and Catalonia in a week."

"Of course I will obey; but it strikes me that the Catalonian method of repairing injustice is somewhat peculiar."

"If you think you have ground for complaint you are at liberty to go   to Madrid and complain to the Court."

"I have certainly grounds enough for complaint, sir, but I shall go to France, and not to Madrid; I have had enough of Spanish justice. Will you please give me the order to leave in writing?"

"That's unnecessary; you may take it for granted. My name is Emmanuel Badillo; I am a secretary of state. That gentleman will escort you back to the room where you were arrested. You will find everything just as you have left it. You are a free man. To-morrow I will send you your passport, signed by the viceroy and myself. Good day, sir."

Accompanied by the officer and a servant bearing my portmanteau, I proceeded to my old inn.

On my way I saw a theatrical poster, and decided to go to the opera. The good landlord was delighted to see me again, and hastened to light me a fire, for a bitterly cold north wind was blowing. He assured me that no one but himself had been in my room, and in the officer's presence he gave me back my sword, my great coat, and, to my astonishment, the hat I had dropped in my flight from the assassins.

The officer asked me if I had any complaints to make, and I replied   that I had none.

"I should like to hear you say that I had done nothing but my duty, and that personally I have not done you any injury."

I shook his hand, and assured him of my esteem.

"Farewell, sir," said he, "I hope you will have a pleasant journey." I told my landlord that I would dine at noon, and that I trusted to him to celebrate my liberation in a fitting manner, and then I went to the post office to see if there were any letters for me. I found five or six letters, with the seals intact, much to my astonishment. What is one to make of a Government which deprives a man of his liberty on some trifling pretext, and, though seizing all his papers, respects the privacy of his letters? But Spain, as I have remarked, is peculiar in every way. These letters were from Paris, Venice, Warsaw, and Madrid, and I have never had any reason to believe that any other letters had come for me during my imprisonment.

I went back to my inn, and asked my landlord to bring the bill.

"You do not owe me anything, sir. Here is your bill for the period preceding your imprisonment, and, as you see, it has been settled. I also received orders from the same source to provide for you during your imprisonment, and as long as you stayed at Barcelona."

"Did you know how long I should remain in prison?"

"No, I was paid by the week."

"Who paid you?"

"You know very well."

"Have you had any note for me?"

"Nothing at all."

"What has become of the valet de place?"

"I paid him, and sent him away immediately after your arrest."

"I should like to have him with me as far as Perpignan."

"You are right, and I think the best thing you can do is to leave Spain altogether, for you will find no justice in it."

"What do they say about my assassination?"

"Why, they say you fired the shot that people heard yourself, and that you made your own sword bloody, for no one was found there, either dead or wounded."

"That's an amusing theory. Where did my hat come from?"

"It was brought to me three days after."

"What a confusion! But was it known that I was imprisoned in the tower?"

"Everybody knew it, and two good reasons were given, the one in public, and the other in private."

"What are these reasons?"

"The public reason was that you had forged your passports; the private one, which was only whispered at the ear, was that you spent all your nights with Nina."

"You might have sworn that I never slept out of your inn."

"I told everyone as much, but no matter; you did go to her house, and for a certain nobleman that's a crime. I am glad you did not fly as I advised you, for as it is your character is cleared before everybody."

"I should like to go to the opera this evening; take me a box."

"It shall be done; but do not have anything more to do with Nina, I entreat you."

"No, my good friend, I have made up my mind to see her no more."

Just as I was sitting down to dinner, a banker's clerk brought me a letter which pleased me very much. It contained the bills of exchange I had drawn in Genoa, in favour of M. Augustin Grimaldi. He now sent them back, with these words:

"Passano has been vainly endeavouring to persuade me to send these bills to Barcelona, so that they may be protested, and you arrested. I now send them to you to convince you that I am not one of those who delight in trampling down the victims of bad fortune.

"—Genoa, November 30th, 1768."

For the fourth time a Genoese had behaved most generously to me. I was almost persuaded that I ought to forgive the infamous Passano for the sake of his four excellent fellow-countrymen.

But this virtue was a little beyond me. I concluded that the best thing I could do would be to rid the Genoese name of the opprobrium which this rascal was always bringing on it, but I could never find an opportunity. Some years after I heard that the wretch died in miserable poverty in Genoa.

I was curious at the time to know what had become of him, as it was important for me to be on my guard. I confided my curiosity to my landlord, and he instructed one of the servants to make enquiries. I only heard the following circumstance:

Ascanio Pogomas, or Passano, had been released at the end of November, and had then been embarked on a felucca bound for Toulon.

The same day I wrote a long and grateful letter to M. Grimaldi. I had indeed reason to be grateful, for if he had listened to my enemy he might have reduced me to a state of dreadful misery.

My landlord had taken the box at the opera in my name, and two hours afterwards, to everyone's great astonishment, the posters announcing the plays of the evening were covered by bills informing the public that two of the performers had been taken ill, that the play would not be given, and the theatre closed till the second day of the new year.

This order undoubtedly came from the viceroy, and everybody knew the reason.

I was sorry to have deprived the people of Barcelona of the only amusement they had in the evening, and resolved to stay indoors, thinking that would be the most dignified course I could adopt.

Petrarch says,—

'Amor che fa gentile un cor villano'.

If he had known the lover of Nina he would have changed the line into

'Amor che fa villan un cor gentile'.

In four months I shall be able to throw some more light on this strange business.

I should have left Barcelona the same day, but a slight tinge of superstition made me desire to leave on the last day of the unhappy year I had spent in Spain. I therefore spent my three days of grace in writing letters to all my friends.

Don Miguel de Cevallos, Don Diego de la Secada, and the Comte de la Peralada came to see me, but separately. Don Diego de la Secada was the uncle of the Countess A—— B—— whom I had met at Milan. These gentlemen told me a tale as strange as any of the circumstances which had happened to me at Barcelona.

On the 26th of December the Abbe Marquisio, the envoy of the Duke of Modena, asked the viceroy, before a considerable number of people, if he could pay me a visit, to give me a letter which he could place in no hands but mine. If not he said he should be obliged to take the letter to Madrid, for which town he was obliged to set out the next day.

The count made no answer, to everyone's astonishment, and the abbe left for Madrid the next day, the eve of my being set at liberty.

I wrote to the abbe, who was unknown to me, but I never succeeded in finding out the truth about this letter.

There could be no doubt that I had been arrested by the despotic viceroy, who had been persuaded by Nina that I was her favoured lover. The question of my passports must have been a mere pretext, for eight or ten days would have sufficed to send them to Madrid and have them back again if their authenticity had been doubted. Possibly Passano might have told the viceroy that any passports of mine were bound to be false, as I should have had to obtain the signature of my own ambassador. This, he might have said, was out of the question as I was in disgrace with the Venetian Government. As a matter of fact, he was mistaken if he really said so, but the mistake would have been an excusable one.

When I made up my mind at the end of August to leave Madrid, I asked the Count of Aranda for a passport. He replied that I must first obtain one from my ambassador, who, he added, could not refuse to do me this service.

Fortified with this opinion I called at the embassy. M. Querini was at San Ildefonso at the time, and I told the porter that I wanted to speak to the secretary of embassy.

The servant sent in my name, and the fop gave himself airs, and pretended that he could not receive me. In my indignation I wrote to him saying that I had not called to pay my court to the secretary, but to demand a passport which was my right. I gave my name and my degree (doctor of law), and begged him to leave the passport with the porter, as I should call for it on the following day.

I presented myself accordingly, and the porter told me that the ambassador had left verbal orders that I was not to have a passport.

I wrote immediately to the Marquis Grimaldi and to the Duke of Lossada, begging them to request the ambassador to send me a passport in the usual form, or else I should publish the shameful reasons for which his uncle Mocenigo had disgraced me.

I do not know whether these gentlemen shewed my letters to Querini, but I do know that the secretary Oliviera sent me my passport.

Thereupon the Count Aranda furnished me with a passport signed by the king.

On the last day of the year I left Barcelona with a servant who sat behind my chaise, and I agreed with my driver to take me to Perpignan by January 3rd, 1769.

The driver was a Piedmontese and a worthy man: The next day he came into the room of the wayside inn where I was dining, and in the presence of my man asked me whether I had any suspicion that I was being followed.

"Well, I may be," I said, "but what makes you ask that question?"

"As you were leaving Barcelona yesterday, I noticed three ill-looking fellows watching us, armed to the teeth. Last night they slept in the stable with my mules. They dined here to-day, and they went on three quarters of an hour ago. They don't speak to anyone, and I don't like the looks of them."

"What shall we do to avoid assassination, or the dread of it?"

"We must start late, and stop at an inn I know of, a league this side of the ordinary stage where they will be awaiting us. If they turn back, and sleep at the same inn as ourselves, we shall be certain."

I thought the idea a sensible one, and we started, I going on foot nearly the whole way; and at five o'clock we halted at a wretched inn, but we saw no signs of the sinister trio.

At eight o'clock I was at supper, when my man came in and told me that the three fellows had come back, and were drinking with our driver in the stable.

My hair stood on end. There could be no more doubt about the matter.

At present, it was true, I had nothing to fear; but it would be getting dark when we arrived at the frontier, and then my peril would come.

I told my servant to shew no sign, but to ask the driver to come and speak with me when the assassins were asleep.

He came at ten o'clock, and told me plainly that we should be all murdered as we approached the French frontier.

"Then you have been drinking with them?"

"Yes, and after we had dispatched a bottle at my expense, one of them asked me why I had not gone on to the end of the stage, where you would be better lodged. I replied that it was late, and you were cold. I might have asked in my turn, why they had not stayed at the stage themselves, and where they were going, but I took care to do nothing of the kind. All I asked was whether the road to Perpignan was a good one, and they told me it was excellent all the way."

"What are they doing now?"

"They are sleeping by my mules, covered with their cloaks."

"What shall we do?"

"We will start at day-break after them, of course, and we shall dine at the usual stage; but after dinner, trust me, we will take a different road, and at midnight we shall be in France safe and sound."

If I could have procured a good armed escort I would not have taken his advice, but in the situation I was in I had no choice.

We found the three scoundrels in the place where the driver had told me we should see them. I gave them a searching glance, and thought they looked like true Sicarii, ready to kill anyone for a little money.

They started in a quarter of an hour, and half an hour later we set out, with a peasant to guide us, and so struck into a cross road. The mules went at a sharp pace, and in seven hours we had done eleven leagues. At ten o'clock we stopped at an inn in a French village, and we had no more to fear. I gave our guide a doubloon, with which he was well pleased, and I enjoyed once more a peaceful night in a French bed, for nowhere will you find such soft beds or such delicious wines as in the good land of France.

The next day I arrived at the posting-inn at Perpignan in time for dinner. I endeavoured in vain to think who could have paid my assassins, but the reader will see the explanation when we get twenty days farther.

At Perpignan I dismissed my driver and my servant, rewarding them according to my ability. I wrote to my brother at Paris, telling him I had had a fortunate escape from the dagger of the assassin. I begged him to direct his answer to Aix, where I intended to spend a fortnight, in the hope of seeing the Marquis d'Argens. I left Perpignan the day after my arrival, and slept at Narbonne, and the day after at Beziers.

The distance from Narbonne to Beziers is only five leagues, and I had not intended to stop; but the good cheer which the kindest of landladies gave me at dinner made me stop with her to supper.

Beziers is a town which looks pleasant even at the worst time of the year. A philosopher who wished to renounce all the vanities of the world, and an Epicurean who would enjoy good cheer cheaply, could find no better retreat than Beziers.

Everybody at Beziers is intelligent, all the women are pretty, and the cooks are all artists; the wines are exquisite—what more could one desire! May its riches never prove its ruin!

When I reached Montpellier, I got down at the "White Horse," with the intention of spending a week there. In the evening I supped at the table d'hote, where I found a numerous company, and I saw to my amusement that for every guest there was a separate dish brought to table.

Nowhere is there better fare than at Montpellier. 'Tis a veritable land of Cocagne!

The next day I breakfasted at the cafe (an institution peculiar to France, the only country where the science of living is really understood), and addressed the first gentleman I met, telling him that I was a stranger and that I would like to know some of the professors. He immediately offered to take me to one of the professors who enjoyed a great reputation.

Herein may be seen another of the good qualities of the French, who rank above other nations by so many titles. To a Frenchman a foreigner is a sacred being; he receives the best of hospitality, not merely in form, but in deed; and his welcome is given with that easy grace which so soon sets a stranger at his ease.

My new friend introduced me to the professor, who received me with all the polished courtesy of the French man of letters. He that loves letters should love all other lovers of letters, and in France that is the case, even more so than Italy. In Germany the literary man has an air of mysterious reserve. He thinks he is proclaiming to all the world that he at all events is a man of no pretension, whereas his pride peeps through every moment. Naturally the stranger is not encouraged by such a manner as this.

At the time of my visit there was an excellent company of actors at Montpellier, whom I went to see the same evening. My bosom swelled at finding myself in the blessed air of France after all the annoyances I had gone through in Spain. I seemed to have become young again; but I was altered, for several beautiful and clever actresses appeared on the stage without arousing any desires within me; and I would have it so.

I had a lively desire to find Madame Castelbajac, not with any wish to renew my old relations with her. I wished to congratulate her on her improved position, but I was afraid of compromising her by asking for her in the town.

I knew that her husband was an apothecary, so I resolved to make the acquaintance of all the apothecaries in the place. I pretended to be in want of some very rare drugs, and entered into conversation about the differences between the trade in France and in foreign countries. If I spoke to the master I hoped he would talk to his wife about the stranger who had visited the countries where she had been, and that that would make her curious to know me. If, on the other hand, I spoke to the man, I knew he would soon tell me all he knew about his master's family.

On the third day my stratagem succeeded. My old friend wrote me a note, telling me that she had seen me speaking to her husband in his shop. She begged me to come again at a certain time, and to tell her husband that I had known her under the name of Mdlle. Blasin in England, Spa, Leipzig, and Vienna, as a seller of lace. She ended her note with these words:

"I have no doubt that my husband will finally introduce you to me as his wife."

I followed her advice, and the good man asked me if I had ever known a young lace seller of the name of Mdlle. Blasin, of Montpellier.

"Yes, I remember her well enough—a delightful and most respectable young woman; but I did not know she came from Montpellier. She was very pretty and very sensible, and I expect she did a good business. I have seen her in several European cities, and the last time at Vienna, where I was able to be of some slight service to her. Her admirable behaviour won her the esteem of all the ladies with whom she came in contact. In England I met her at the house of a duchess."

"Do you think you would recognize her if you saw her again?"

"By Jove! I should think so! But is she at Montpellier? If so, tell her that the Chevalier de Seingalt is here."

"Sir, you shall speak to her yourself, if you will do me the honour to follow me."

My heart leapt, but I restrained myself. The worthy apothecary went through the shop, climbed a stair, and, opening a door on the first floor, said to me,—

"There she is."

"What, mademoiselle! You here? I am delighted to see you."

"This is not a young lady, sir, 'tis my dear wife; but I hope that will not hinder you from embracing her."

"I have never had such an honour; but I will avail myself of your permission with pleasure. Then you have got married at Montpellier. I congratulate both of you, and wish you all health and happiness. Tell me, did you have a pleasant journey from Vienna to Lyons?"

Madame Blasin (for so I must continue to designate her) answered my question according to her fancy, and found me as good an actor as she was an actress.

We were very glad to see each other again, but the apothecary was delighted at the great respect with which I treated his wife.

For a whole hour we carried on a conversation of a perfectly imaginary character, and with all the simplicity of perfect truth.

She asked me if I thought of spending the carnival at Montpellier, and seemed quite mortified when I said that I thought of going on the next day.

Her husband hastened to say that that was quite out of the question.

"Oh, I hope you won't go," she added, "you must do my husband the honour of dining with us."

After the husband had pressed me for some time I gave in, and accepted their invitation to dinner for the day after next.

Instead of stopping two days I stopped four. I was much pleased with the husband's mother, who was advanced in years but extremely intelligent. She had evidently made a point of forgetting everything unpleasant in the past history of her son's wife.

Madame Blasin told me in private that she was perfectly happy, and I had every reason to believe that she was speaking the truth. She had made a rule to be most precise in fulfilling her wifely duties, and rarely went out unless accompanied by her husband or her mother-in-law.

I spent these four days in the enjoyment of pure and innocent friendship without there being the slightest desire on either side to renew our guilty pleasures.

On the third day after I had dined with her and her husband, she told me, while we were alone for a moment, that if I wanted fifty louis she knew where to get them for me. I told her to keep them for another time, if I was so happy as to see her again, and so unhappy as to be in want.

I left Montpellier feeling certain that my visit had increased the esteem in which her husband and her mother-in-law held her, and I congratulated myself on my ability to be happy without committing any sins.

The day after I had bade them farewell, I slept at Nimes, where I spent three days in the company of a naturalist: M. de Seguier, the friend of the Marquis Maffei of Verona. In his cabinet of natural history I saw and admired the immensity and infinity of the Creator's handiwork.

Nimes is a town well worthy of the stranger's observation; it provides food for the mind, and the fair sex, which is really fair there, should give the heart the food it likes best.

I was asked to a ball, where, as a foreigner, I took first place—a privilege peculiar to France, for in England, and still more in Spain, a foreigner means an enemy.

On leaving Nimes I resolved to spend the carnival at Aix, where the nobility is of the most distinguished character. I believe I lodged at the "Three Dolphins," where I found a Spanish cardinal on his way to Rome to elect a successor to Pope Rezzonico.

CHAPTER IX

My Stay at Aix; I Fall Ill—I am Cared for By an Unknown Lady—The Marquis d'Argens—Cagliostro

My room was only separated from his Castilian eminence's by a light partition, and I could hear him quite plainly reprimanding his chief servant for being too economical.

"My lord, I do my best, but it is really impossible to spend more, unless I compel the inn-keepers to take double the amount of their bills; and your eminence will admit that nothing in the way of rich and expensive dishes has been spared."

"That may be, but you ought to use your wits a little; you might for example order meals when we shall not require any. Take care that there are always three tables—one for us, one for my officers, and the third for the servants. Why I see that you only give the postillions a franc over the legal charge, I really blush for you; you must give them a crown extra at least. When they give you change for a louis, leave it on the table; to put back one's change in one's pocket is an action only worthy of a beggar. They will be saying at Versailles and Madrid, and maybe at Rome itself, that the Cardinal de la Cerda is a miser. I am no such thing, and I do not want to be thought one. You must really cease to dishonour me, or leave my service."

A year before this speech would have astonished me beyond measure, but now I was not surprised, for I had acquired some knowledge of Spanish manners. I might admire the Senor de la Cerda's prodigality, but I could not help deploring such ostentation on the part of a Prince of the Church about to participate in such a solemn function.

What I had heard him say made me curious to see him, and I kept on the watch for the moment of his departure. What a man! He was not only ill made, short and sun-burnt; but his face was so ugly and so low that I concluded that AEsop himself must have been a little Love beside his eminence. I understood now why he was so profuse in his generosity and decorations, for otherwise he might well have been taken for a stableboy. If the conclave took the eccentric whim of making him pope, Christ would never have an uglier vicar.

I enquired about the Marquis d'Argens soon after the departure of his eminence, and was told that he was in the country with his brother, the Marquis d'Eguille, President of the Parliament, so I went there.

This marquis, famous for his friendship for Frederick II. rather than for his writings (which are no longer read), was an old man when I saw him. He was a worthy man, fond of pleasure, a thorough-paced Epicurean, and had married an actress named Cochois, who had proved worthy of the honour he had laid on her. He was deeply learned and had a thorough knowledge of Latin, Greek, and Hebrew literature. His memory was prodigious.

He received me very well, and recalled what his friend the marshal had written about me. He introduced me to his wife and to his brother, a distinguished jurist, a man of letters, and a strictly moral man by temperament as much as religion. Though a highly intellectual man, he was deeply and sincerely religious.

He was very fond of his brother, and grieved for his irreligion, but hoped that grace would eventually bring him back to the fold of the Church. His brother encouraged him in his hopes, while laughing at them in private, but as they were both sensible men they never discussed religion together.

I was introduced to a numerous company of both sexes, chiefly consisting of relations. All were amiable and highly polished, like all the Provencal nobility.

Plays were performed on the miniature stage, good cheer prevailed, and at intervals we walked in the garden, in spite of the weather. In Province, however, the winter is only severe when the wind blows from the north, which unfortunately often happens.

Among the company were a Berlin lady (widow of the marquis's nephew) and her brother. This young gentleman, who was gay and free from care, enjoyed all the pleasures of the house without paying any attention to the religious services which were held every day. If he thought on the matter at all, he was a heretic; and when the Jesuit chaplain was saying mass he amused himself by playing on the flute; he laughed at everything. He was unlike his sister, who had not only become a Catholic, but was a very devout one. She was only twenty-two.

Her brother told me that her husband, who had died of consumption, and whose mind was perfectly clear to the last, as is usually the case in phthisis, had told her that he could not entertain any hopes of seeing her in the other world unless she became a Catholic.

These words were engraved on her heart; she had adored her husband, and she resolved to leave Berlin to live with his relations. No one ventured to oppose this design, her brother accompanying her, and she was welcomed joyfully by all her husband's kinsfolk.

This budding saint was decidedly plain.

Her brother, finding me less strict than the others, soon constituted himself my friend. He came over to Aix every day, and took me to the houses of all the best people.

We were at least thirty at table every day, the dishes were delicate without undue profusion, the conversation gay and animated without any improprieties. I noticed that whenever the Marquis d'Argens chanced to let slip any equivocal expressions, all the ladies made wry faces, and the chaplain hastened to turn the conversation. This chaplain had nothing jesuitical in his appearance; he dressed in the costume of an ordinary priest, and I should never had known him if the Marquis d'Argens had not warned me. However, I did not allow his presence to act as a wet blanket.

I told, in the most decent manner possible, the story of the picture of the Virgin suckling her Divine Child, and how the Spaniards deserted the chapel after a stupid priest had covered the beautiful breast with a kerchief. I do not know how it was, but all the ladies began to laugh. The disciple of Loyola was so displeased at their mirth, that he took upon himself to tell me that it was unbecoming to tell such equivocal stories in public. I thanked him by an inclination of the head, and the Marquis d'Argens, by way of turning the conversation, asked me what was the Italian for a splendid dish of stewed veal, which Madame d'Argens was helping.

"Una crostata," I replied, "but I really do not know the Italian for the 'beatilles' with which it is stuffed."

These 'beatilles' were balls of rice, veal, champignons, artichoke, foie gras, etc.

The Jesuit declared that in calling them 'beatilles' I was making a mock of the glories of hereafter.

I could not help roaring with laughter at this, and the Marquis d'Eguille took my part, and said that 'beatilles' was the proper French for these balls.

After this daring difference of opinion with his director, the worthy man thought it would be best to talk of something else. Unhappily, however, he fell out of the frying-pan into the fire by asking me my opinion as to the election of the next pope.

"I believe it will be Ganganelli," I replied, "as he is the only monk in the conclave."

"Why should it be necessary to choose a monk?"

"Because none but a monk would dare to commit the excess which the

Spaniards will demand of the new pope."

"You mean the suppression of the Jesuits."

"Exactly."

"They will never obtain such a demand."

"I hope not, for the Jesuits were my masters, and I love them accordingly. But all the same Ganganelli will be elected, for an amusing and yet a weighty reason."

"Tell us the reason."

"He is the only cardinal who does not wear a wig; and you must consider that since the foundation of the Holy See the Pope has never been bewigged."

This reason created a great deal of amusement; but the conversation was brought back to the suppression of the Jesuits, and when I told the company that I had heard from the Abbe Pinzi I saw the Jesuit turn pale.

"The Pope could never suppress the order," he said.

"It seems that you have never been at a Jesuit seminary," I replied, "for the dogma of the order is that the Pope can do everything, 'et aliquid pluris'."

This answer made everybody suppose me to be unaware that I was speaking to a Jesuit, and as he gave me no answer the topic was abandoned.

After dinner I was asked to stay and see 'Polieucte' played; but I excused myself, and returned to Aix with the young Berliner, who told me the story of his sister, and made me acquainted with the character of the society to which the Marquis d'Eguille was chiefly addicted. I felt that I could never adapt myself to their prejudices, and if it had not been for my young friend, who introduced me to some charming people, I should have gone on to Marseilles.

What with assemblies, balls, suppers, and the society of the handsome Provençal ladies, I managed to spend the whole of the carnival and a part of Lent at Aix.

I had made a present of a copy of the "Iliad" to the learned Marquis d'Argens; to his daughter, who was also a good scholar, I gave a Latin tragedy.

The "Iliad" had Porphyry's comment; it was a copy of a rare edition, and was richly bound.

As the marquis came to Aix to thank me, I had to pay another visit to the country house.

In the evening I drove back in an open carriage. I had no cloak, and a cold north wind was blowing; I was perishing with cold, but instead of going to bed at once I accompanied the Berliner to the house of a woman who had a daughter of the utmost beauty. Though the girl was only fourteen, she had all the indications of the marriageable age, and yet none of the Provencal amateurs had succeeded in making her see daylight. My friend had already made several unsuccessful efforts. I laughed at him, as I knew it was all a cheat, and I followed him to the house with the idea of making the young imposter dismount from her high horse, as I had done in similar cases in England and Metz.

We set to work; and, far from resisting, the girl said she would be only too glad to get rid of the troublesome burden.

I saw that the difficulty only proceeded from the way she held herself, and I ought to have whipped her, as I had done in Venice twenty-five years ago, but I was foolish enough to try to take the citadel by storm. But my age of miracles was gone.

I wearied myself to no purpose for a couple of hours, and then went to my inn, leaving the young Prussian to do his best.

I went to bed with a pain in my side, and after six hours' sleep awoke feeling thoroughly ill. I had pleurisy. My landlord called in an old doctor, who refused to let me blood. A severe cough came on, and the next day I began to spit blood. In six or seven days the malady became so serious that I was confessed and received the last sacraments.

On the tenth day, the disease having abated for three days, my clever old doctor answered for my life, but I continued to spit blood till the eighteenth day.

My convalescence lasted for three weeks, and I found it more trying than the actual illness, for a man in pain has no time to grow weary. Throughout the whole case I was tended day and night by a strange woman, of whom I knew nothing. She nursed me with the tenderest care, and I awaited my recovery to give her my sincere thanks.

She was not an old woman, neither was she attractive looking. She had slept in my room all the time. After Eastertide, feeling I was well enough to venture out, I thanked her to the best of my ability, and asked who had sent her to me. She told me it was the doctor, and so bade me farewell.

A few days later I was thanking my old doctor for having procured me such a capital nurse, but he stared at me and said he knew nothing about the woman.

I was puzzled, and asked my landlord if she could throw any light on the strange nurse's identity; but she knew nothing, and her ignorance seemed universal. I could not discover whence or how she came to attend me.

After my convalescence I took care to get all the letters which had been awaiting me, and amongst them was a letter from my brother in Paris, in answer to the epistle I wrote him from Perpignan. He acknowledged my letter, and told me how delighted he had been to receive it, after hearing the dreadful news that I had been assassinated on the borders of Catalonia at the beginning of January.

"The person who gave me the news," my brother added, "was one of your best friends, Count Manucci, an attache at the Venetian embassy. He said there could be no doubt as to the truth of the report."

This letter was like a flash of lightning to me. This friend of mine had pushed his vengeance so far as to pay assassins to deprive me of my life.

Manucci had gone a little too far.

He must have been pretty well qualified to prophesy, as he was so certain of my death. He might have known that in thus proclaiming in advance the manner of my death, he was also proclaiming himself as my murderer.

I met him at Rome, two years later, and when I would have made him confess his guilt, he denied everything, saying he had received the news from Barcelona; however, we will speak of this in its proper place.

I dined and supped every day at the table d'hote, and one day I heard the company talking of a male and female pilgrim who had recently arrived. They were Italians, and were returning from St. James of Compostella. They were said to be high-born folks, as they had distributed large alms on their entry into the town.

It was said that the female pilgrim, who had gone to bed on her arrival, was charming. They were staying at the same inn as I was, and we all got very curious about them.

As an Italian, I put myself at the head of the band who proceeded to call on the pilgrims, who, in my opinion, must either be fanatics or rogues.

We found the lady sitting in an arm-chair, looking very tired. She was young, beautiful, and melancholy-looking, and in her hands she held a brass crucifix some six inches long. She laid it down when we came in, and got up and received us most graciously. Her companion, who was arranging cockle-shells on his black mantle, did not stir; he seemed to say, by glancing at his wife, that we must confine our attentions to her. He seemed a man of twenty-four or twenty-five years of age. He was short and badly hung, and his face bore all the indications of daring, impudence, sarcasm, and imposture. His wife, on the other hand, was all meekness and simplicity, and had that modesty which adds so much to the charm of feminine beauty. They only spoke just enough French to make themselves understood on their journey, and when they heard me addressing them in Italian they seemed much relieved.

The lady told me she was a Roman, but I could have guessed as much from her accent. I judged the man to be a Neapolitan or Sicilian. Their passport, dated Rome, called him Balsamo, while she bore the names of Serafina Feliciani, which she still retains. Ten years later we shall hear more of this couple under the name of Cagliostro.

"We are going back to Rome," said she, "well pleased with our devotions to St. James of Compostella and to Our Lady del Pilar. We have walked the whole way on foot, living on alms, so as to more surely win the mercy of the God whom I have offended so grievously. We have had silver, and even gold money given us, and in every town we came to we gave what remained to the poor, so as not to offend God by lack of faith.

"My husband is strong, and has not suffered much, but I have found so much walking very fatiguing. We have slept on straw or bad beds, always with our clothes on, to avoid contracting diseases it would be hard to rid one's self of."

It seemed to me that this last circumstance was added to make us wish to find out whether the rest of her body could compare with her hands and arms in whiteness.

"Do you think of making any stay?"

"My weariness will oblige us to stay here for three days; then we shall go to Rome by the way of Turin, where we shall pay our devotion to the Holy Sudary."

"You know, of course, that there are several of them in Europe."

"So we have heard, but we are assured that the Sudary of Turin is the true one. It is the kerchief with which St. Veronica wiped the face of Our Lord, who left the imprint of His divine face upon it."

We left them, well pleased with the appearance and manners of the lady pilgrim, but placing very little trust in her devotion. I was still weak from my illness, and she inspired me with no desires, but the rest would have gladly supped with her if they had thought there was anything to follow.

Next day her husband asked me if I would come up and breakfast with them, or if they should come down and breakfast with me. It would have been impolite to have replied neither, so I said that I should be delighted to see them in my room.

At breakfast I asked the pilgrim what he did, and he replied that he was an artist.

He could not design a picture, but he could copy it, and he assured me that he could copy an engraving so exactly that none could tell the copy from the original.

"I congratulate you. If you are not a rich man, you are, at least, certain of earning a living with this talent."

"Everybody says the same, but it is a mistake. I have pursued this craft at Rome and at Naples, and found I had to work all day to make half a tester, and that's not enough to live on."

He then shewed me some fans he had done, and I thought them most beautiful. They were done in pen and ink, and the finest copper-plate could not have surpassed them.

Next he showed me a copy from a Rembrandt, which if anything, was finer than the original. In spite of all he swore that the work he got barely supported him, but I did not believe what he said. He was a weak genius who preferred a vagabond life to methodical labour.

I offered a Louis for one of his fans, but he refused to take it, begging me to accept the fan as a gift, and to make a collection for him at the table d'hote, as he wanted to start the day after next.

I accepted the present and promised to do as he desired, and succeeded in making up a purse of two hundred francs for them.

The woman had the most virtuous air. She was asked to write her name on a lottery ticket, but refused, saying that no honest girls were taught to write at Rome.

Everybody laughed at this excuse except myself, and I pitied her, as I could see that she was of very low origin.

Next day she came and asked me to give her a letter of introduction for Avignon. I wrote her out two; one to M. Audifret the banker, and the other to the landlady of the inn. In the evening she returned me the letter to the banker, saying that it was not necessary for their purposes. At the same time she asked me to examine the letter closely, to see if it was really the same document I had given her. I did so, and said I was sure it was my letter.

She laughed, and told me I was mistaken as it was only a copy.

"Impossible!"

She called her husband, who came with the letter in his hand.

I could doubt no longer, and said to him,—

"You are a man of talents, for it is much harder to imitate a handwriting than an engraving. You ought to make this talent serve you in good stead; but be careful, or it may cost you your life."

The next day the couple left Aix. In ten years I saw them again under the name of Count and Countess Pellegrini.

At the present period he is in a prison which he will probably never leave, and his wife is happy, maybe, in a convent.

CHAPTER X

My Departure—Letter from Henriette—Marsellies—History of Nina—Nice—Turin—Lugano—Madame De****

As soon as I had regained my usual strength, I went to take leave of the Marquis d'Argens and his brother. I dined with them, pretending not to observe the presence of the Jesuit, and I then spent three delightful hours in conversation with the learned and amiable Marquis d'Argens. He told me a number of interesting anecdotes about the private life of Frederick II. No doubt the reader would like to have them, but I lack the energy to set them down. Perhaps some other day when the mists about Dux have dispersed, and some rays of the sun shine in upon me, I shall commit all these anecdotes to paper, but now I have not the courage to do so.

Frederick had his good and his bad qualities, like all great men, but when every deduction on the score of his failings has been made, he still remains the noblest figure in the eighteenth century.

The King of Sweden, who has been assassinated, loved to excite hatred that he might have the glory of defying it to do its worst. He was a despot at heart, and he came to a despot's end. He might have foreseen a violent death, for throughout his life he was always provoking men to the point of despair. There can be no comparison between him and Frederick.

The Marquis d'Argens made me a present of all his works, and on my asking him if I could congratulate myself on possessing the whole number, he said yes, with the exception of a fragment of autobiography which he had written in his youth, and which he had afterwards suppressed.

"Why so?" I asked.

"Because I was foolish enough to write the truth. Never give way to this temptation, if it assails you. If you once begin on this plan you are not only compelled to record all your vices and follies, but to treat them in the severe tone of a philosophical historian. You must not, of course, omit the good you may have done; and so praise and blame is mingled on every page. All the evil you say of yourself will be held for gospel, your peccadilloes will be made into crimes, and your good deeds will not only be received with incredulity, but you will be taxed with pride and vanity for having recorded them. Besides, if you write your memoirs, you make an enemy in every chapter if you once begin to tell the truth. A man should neither talk of himself nor write of himself, unless it be to refute some calumny or libel."

I was convinced, and promised never to be guilty of such a folly, but in spite of that I have been writing memoirs for the last seven years, and though I repent of having begun, I have sworn to go on to the end. However, I write in the hope that my Memoirs may never see the light of day; in the first place the censure would not allow them to be printed, and in the second I hope I shall be strong-minded enough, when my last illness comes, to have all my papers burnt before my eyes. If that be not the case I count on the indulgence of my readers, who should remember that I have only written my story to prevent my going mad in the midst of all the petty insults and disagreeables which I have to bear day by day from the envious rascals who live with me in this castle of Count Waldstein, or Wallenstein, at Dux.

I write ten or twelve hours a day, and so keep black melancholy at bay. My readers shall hear more of my sufferings later on, if I do not die before I write them down.

The day after Corpus Christi I left Aix for Marseilles. But here I must set down a circumstance that I had forgotten; I mean the procession of Corpus Christi.

Everyone knows that this festival is celebrated with great ceremony all over Christendom; but at Aix these ceremonies are of such a nature that every man of sense must be shocked at my recital.

It is well known that this procession in honour of the Being of beings, represented under the sacramental forms, is followed by all the religious confraternities, and this is duly done at Aix; but the scandalous part of the ceremony is the folly and the buffoonery which is allowed in a rite which should be designed to stir up the hearts of men to awe and reverence their Creator.

Instead of that, the devil, death, and the seven deadly sins, are impersonated in the procession. They are clad in the most absurd costumes, and make hideous contortions, beating and abusing each other in their supposed vexation at having to join in the Creator's praises. The people hoot and hiss them, the lower classes sing songs in derision of them, and play them all manner of tricks, and the whole scene is one of incredible noise, uproar, and confusion, more worthy of some pagan bacchanalia than a procession of Christian people. All the country-folk from five or six leagues around Aix pour into the town on that day to do honour to God. It is the only occasion of the kind, and the clergy, either knavish or ignorant, encourage all this shameful riot. The lower orders take it all in good faith, and anyone who raised any objection would run some risk, for the bishop goes in front of the saturnalia, and consequently it is all holy.

I expressed my disapproval of the whole affair, as likely to bring discredit on religion, to a councillor of parliament, M. de St. Marc; but he told me gravely that it was an excellent thing, as it brought no less than a hundred thousand francs into the town on the single day.

I could find no reply to this very weighty reason.

Every day I spent at Aix I thought of Henriette. I knew her real name, and remembering the message she had sent me by Marcoline I hoped to meet her in some assembly, being ready to adapt my conduct to hers. I had often heard her name mentioned, but I never allowed myself to ask any question, not wishing our old friendship to be suspected. Believing her to be at her country house, I had resolved on paying her a visit, and had only stayed on at Aix so as to recover my health before seeing her. In due course I left Aix with a letter in my pocket for her, resolving to send it in, and to remain in my carriage till she asked me to get down.

We arrived at her residence at eleven o'clock. A man came to the door, took my letter, and said madam should have it without fail.

"Then she is not here."

"No, sir; she is at Aix."

"Since when?"

"For the last six months."

"Where does she live?"

"In her town house. She will be coming here in three weeks to spend the summer as usual."

"Will you let me write a letter?"

"If you will get down you will find all the necessary materials in madam's room."

I went into the house, and to my extreme surprise found myself face to face with my nurse.

"You live here, then."

"Yes, sir."

"Since when?"

"For the last ten years."

"How did you come to nurse me?"

"If you will step upstairs I will tell you."

Her story was as follows:

"Madam sent for me in haste, and told me to go and attend to you as if it were herself. She told me to say that the doctor had sent me if you asked any questions."

"The doctor said he didn't know you."

"Perhaps he was speaking the truth, but most likely he had received orders from madam. That's all I know, but I wonder you haven't seen her at Aix."

"She cannot see any company, for I have been everywhere."

"She does not see any company at her own house, but she goes everywhere."

"It's very strange. I must have seen her, and yet I do not think I could have passed her by unrecognized. You have been with her ten years?"

"Yes, sir, as I had the honour of informing you."

"Has she changed? Has she had any sickness? Has she aged?"

"Not at all. She has become rather stout, but I assure you you would take her for a woman of thirty."

"I must be blind, or I cannot have seen her. I am going to write to her now."

The woman went out, leaving me in astonishment, at the extraordinary situation in which I was placed.

"Ought I to return to Aix immediately?" I asked myself. She has a town house, but does not see company, but she might surely see me: She loves me still. She cared for me all through my illness, and she would not have done so if she had become indifferent to me. She will be hurt at my not recognizing her. She must know that I have left Aix, and will no doubt guess that I am here now. Shall I go to her or shall I write? I resolved to write, and I told her in my letter that I should await her reply at Marseilles. I gave the letter to my late nurse, with some money to insure its being dispatched at once, and drove on to Marseilles where I alighted at an obscure inn, not wishing to be recognized. I had scarcely got out of my carriage when I saw Madame Schizza, Nina's sister. She had left Barcelona with her husband. They had been at Marseilles three or four days and were going to Leghorn.

Madame Schizza was alone at the moment, her husband having gone out; and as I was full of curiosity I begged her to come up to my room while my dinner was getting ready.

"What is your sister doing? Is she still at Barcelona?"

"Yes; but she will not be there long, for the bishop will not have her in the town or the diocese, and the bishop is stronger than the viceroy. She only returned to Barcelona on the plea that she wished to pass through Catalonia of her way home, but she does not need to stay there for nine or ten months on that account. She will have to leave in a month for certain, but she is not much put out, as the viceroy is sure to keep her wherever she goes, and she may eventually succeed in ruining him. In the meanwhile she is revelling in the bad repute she has gained for her lover."

"I know something of her peculiarities; but she cannot dislike a man who has made her rich."

"Rich! She has only got her diamonds. Do you imagine this monster capable of any feelings of gratitude? She is not a human being, and no one knows her as I do. She has made the count commit a hundred acts of injustice so that all Spain may talk of her, and know that she has made herself mistress of his body and soul, and all he has. The worse his actions are, the more certain she feels that people will talk of her, and that is all she wants. Her obligations to me are beyond counting, for she owes me all, even to her existence, and instead of continuing my husband in her service she has sent him about his business."

"Then I wonder how she came to treat me so generously."

"If you knew all, you would not feel grateful to her."

"Tell me all, then."

"She only paid for your keep at the inn and in prison to make people believe you were her lover, and to shame the count. All Barcelona knows that you were assassinated at her door, and that you were fortunate enough to run the fellow through."

"But she cannot have been the instigator of, or even the accomplice in, the plot for my assassination. That's against nature."

"I dare say, but everything in Nina is against nature. What I tell you is the bare truth, for I was a witness of it all. Whenever the viceroy visited her she wearied him with praise of your gallantry, your wit, your noble actions, comparing you with the Spaniards, greatly to their disadvantage.

"The count got impatient and told her to talk of something else, but she would not; and at last he went away, cursing your name. Two days before you came to grief he left her, saying,—

"'Valga me Dios! I will give you a pleasure you do not expect.'

"I assure you that when we heard the pistol-shot after you had gone, she remarked, without evincing the slightest emotion, that the shot was the pleasure her rascally Spaniard had promised her.

"I said that you might be killed.

"'All the worse for the count,' she replied, 'for his turn will come also.'

"Then she began laughing like a madcap; she was thinking of the excitement your death would cause in Barcelona.

"At eight o'clock the following day, your man came and told her that you had been taken to the citadel; and I will say it to her credit, she seemed relieved to hear you were alive."

"My man—I did not know that he was in correspondence with her."

"No, I suppose not; but I assure you the worthy man was very much attached to you."

"I am sure he was. Go on."

"Nina then wrote a note to your landlord. She did not shew it me, but it no doubt contained instructions to supply you with everything.

"The man told us that he had seen your sword all red with blood, and that your cloak had a bullet hole through it. She was delighted, but do not think it was because she loved you; she was glad you had escaped that you might take your revenge. However, she was troubled by the pretext on which the count had had you arrested.

"Ricla did not come to see her that day, but he came the next day at eight o'clock, and the infamous creature received him with a smiling face. She told him she had heard he had imprisoned you, and that she was obliged to him, as he had, of course, done so to protect you from any fresh attempts on your life.

"He answered, dryly, that your arrest had nothing to do with anything that might have happened the night before. He added that you had only been seized pending the examination of your papers, and that if they were found to be in good form, you would be set at liberty in the course of a few days.

"Nina asked him who was the man that you had wounded. He replied that the police were enquiring into the matter, but that so far they had neither found a dead man nor a wounded man, nor any traces of blood. All that had been found was Casanova's hat, and this had been returned to him.

"I left them alone together till midnight, so I cannot say what further converse they may have had on the subject, but three or four days later everybody knew that you were imprisoned in the tower.

"Nina asked the count the reason of this severity in the evening, and he replied that your passports were thought to be forgeries, because you were in disgrace with the State Inquisitors, and therefore would not be in a position to get a passport from the Venetian ambassador. On this supposition he said you had been placed in the tower, and if it proved to be a true one, you would be still more severely punished.

"This news disturbed us, and when we heard that Pogomas had been arrested we felt certain he had denounced you in revenge for your having procured his dismissal from Nina's house. When we heard that he had been let out and sent to Genoa, we expected to hear of your being set at liberty, as the authorities must have been satisfied of the genuine character of your passports; but you were still shut up, and Nina did not know what to think, and the count would not answer her when she made enquiries about you. She had made up her mind to say no more about it, when at last we heard you had been set free and that your passports had been declared genuine.

"Nina thought to see you in the pit of the opera-house, and made preparations for a triumph in her box; but she was in despair when she heard no performance was to be given. In the evening the count told her that your passports had been returned with the order to leave in three days. The false creature praised her lover's prudence to his face, but she cursed him in her heart.

"She knew you would not dare to see her, and when you left without writing her a note, she said you had received secret orders not to hold any further communications with her. She was furious with the viceroy.

"'If Casanova had had the courage to ask me to go with him, I would have gone,' said she.

"Your man told her of your fortunate escape from three assassins. In the evening she congratulated Ricla on the circumstance, but he swore he knew nothing about it. Nina did not believe him. You may thank God from the bottom of your heart that you ever left Spain alive after knowing Nina. She would have cost you your life at last, and she punishes me for having given her life."

"What! Are you her mother?"

"Yes; Nina, that horrible woman, is my daughter."

"Really? Everybody says you are her sister."

"That is the horrible part of it, everybody is right."

"Explain yourself!"

"Yes, though it is to my shame. She is my sister and my daughter, for she is the daughter of my father."

"What! your father loved you?"

"I do not know whether the scoundrel loved me, but he treated me as his wife. I was sixteen then. She is the daughter of the crime, and God knows she is sufficient punishment for it. My father died to escape her vengeance; may he also escape the vengeance of God. I should have strangled her in her cradle, but maybe I shall strangle her yet. If I do not, she will kill me."

I remained dumb at the conclusion of this dreadful story, which bore all the marks of truth.

"Does Nina know that you are her mother?"

"Her own father told her the secret when she was twelve, after he had initiated her into the life she has been living ever since. He would have made her a mother in her turn if he had not killed himself the same year, maybe to escape the gallows."

"How did the Conte de Ricla fall in love with her?"

"It is a short story and a curious one. Two years ago she came to Barcelona from Portugal, and was placed in one of the ballets for the sake of her pretty face, for as to talents she had none, and could only do the rebaltade (a sort of skip and pirouette) properly.

"The first evening she danced she was loudly applauded by the pit, for as she did the rebaltade she shewed her drawers up to her waist. In Spain any actress who shews her drawers on the stage is liable to a fine of a crown. Nina knew nothing about this, and, hearing the applause, treated the audience to another skip of the same kind, but at the end of the ballet she was told to pay two crowns for her immodesty. Nina cursed and swore, but she had to give in. What do you think she did to elude the law, and at the same time avenge herself?"

"Danced badly, perhaps."

"She danced without any drawers at all, and did her rebdltade as before, which caused such an effervescence of high spirits in the house as had never been known at Barcelona.

"The Conte de Ricla had seen her from his box, and was divided between horror and admiration, and sent for the inspector to tell him that this impudent creature must be punished.

"'In the mean time,' said he, 'bring her before me.'

"Presently Nina appeared in the viceroy's box, and asked him, impudently, what he wanted with her.

"'You are an immodest woman, and have failed in your duty to the public.'

"'What have I done?

"'You performed the same skip as before.'

"'Yes, but I haven't broken your law, for no one can have seen my drawers as I took the precaution not to put any on. What more can I do for your cursed law, which has cost me two crowns already? Just tell me.'

"The viceroy and the great personages around him had much ado to refrain from laughter, for Nina was really in the right, and a serious discussion of the violated law would have been ridiculous.

"The viceroy felt he was in a false position, and merely said that if she ever danced without drawers again she should have a month's imprisonment on bread and water.

"A week after one of my husband's ballets was given. It was so well received that the audience encored it with enthusiasm. Ricla gave orders that the public should be satisfied, and all the dancers were told they would have to reappear.

"Nina, who was almost undressed, told my husband to do as best he could, as she was not going to dance again. As she had the chief part my husband could not do without her, and sent the manager to her dressing-room. She pushed the poor man out with so much violence that he fell against the wall of the passage, head foremost.

"The manager told his piteous tale to the viceroy, who ordered two soldiers to bring her before him. This was his ruin; for Nina is a beautiful woman, and in her then state of undress she would have seduced the coldest of men.

"The count reproved her, but his voice and his manner were ill-assured, and growing bolder as she watched his embarrassment, Nina replied that he might have her torn to pieces if he liked, but she would not dance against her will, and nowhere in her agreement was it stipulated that she should dance twice in the same evening, whether for his pleasure or anyone else's. She also expressed her anger at making her appear before him in a state of semi-nudity, and swore she would never forgive his barbarous and despotic conduct.

"'I will dance no more before you or your people. Let me go away, or kill me if you like; do your worst on me, and you shall find that I am a Venetian and a free woman!'

"The viceroy sat astonished, and said she must be mad. He then summoned my husband and told him she was no longer in his service. Nina was told she was free, and could go where she would.

"She went back to her dressing-room and came to us, where she was living.

"The ballet went on without her, and the poor viceroy sat in a dream, for the poison had entered into his veins.

"Next day a wretched singer named Molinari called on Nina and told her that the viceroy was anxious to know whether she were really mad or not, and would like to see her in a country house, the name of which he mentioned: this was just what the wretched woman wanted.

"'Tell his highness,' she said to Molinari, 'that I will come, and that he will find me as gentle as a lamb and as good as an angel.'

"This is the way in which the connection began, and she fathomed his character so astutely that she maintained her conquest as much with ill-treatment and severity as with her favours."

Such was the tale of the hapless Madame Schizza. It was told with all the passion of an Italian divided between repentance for the past and the desire of vengeance.

The next day, as I had expected, I received a letter from Henriette. It ran as follows:

"My Dear Old Friend,—Nothing could be more romantic than our meeting at my country house six years ago, and now again, after a parting of so many years. Naturally we have both grown older, and though I love you still I am glad you did not recognize me. Not that I have become ugly, but I am stout, and this gives me another look. I am a widow, and well enough off to tell you that if you lack money you will find some ready for you in Henriette's purse. Do not come back to Aix to see me, as your return might give rise to gossip; but if you chance to come here again after some time, we may meet, though not as old acquaintances. I am happy to think that I have perhaps prolonged your days by giving you a nurse for whose trustworthiness I would answer. If you would like to correspond with me I should be happy to do my part. I am very curious to know what happened to you after your flight from The Leads, and after the proofs you have given me of your discretion I think I shall be able to tell you how we came to meet at Cesena, and how I returned to my country. The first part is a secret for everyone; only M. d'Antoine is acquainted with a portion of the story. I am grateful for the reticence you have observed, though Marcoline must have delivered the message I gave her. Tell me what has become of that beautiful girl. Farewell!"

I replied, accepting her offer to correspond, and I told her the whole story of my adventures. From her I received forty letters, in which the history of her life is given. If she die before me, I shall add these letters to my Memoirs, but at present she is alive and happy, though advanced in years.

The day after I went to call on Madame Audibert, and we went together to see Madame N—— N——, who was already the mother of three children. Her husband adored her, and she was very happy. I gave her good news of Marcoline, and told the story of Croce and Charlotte's death, which affected her to tears.

In turn she told me about Rosalie, who was quite a rich woman. I had no hopes of seeing her again, for she lived at Genoa, and I should not have cared to face M. Grimaldi.

My niece (as I once called her) mortified me unintentionally; she said I was ageing. Though a man can easily make a jest of his advancing years, a speech like this is not pleasant when one has not abandoned the pursuit of pleasure. She gave me a capital dinner, and her husband made me offers which I was ashamed to accept. I had fifty Louis, and, intending to go on to Turin, I did not feel uneasy about the future.

At Marseilles I met the Duc de Vilardi, who was kept alive by the art of Tronchin. This nobleman, who was Governor of Provence, asked me to supper, and I was surprised to meet at his house the self-styled Marquis d'Aragon; he was engaged in holding the bank. I staked a few coins and lost, and the marquis asked me to dine with him and his wife, an elderly Englishwoman, who had brought him a dowry of forty thousand guineas absolutely, with twenty thousand guineas which would ultimately go to her son in London. I was not ashamed to borrow fifty Louis from this lucky rascal, though I felt almost certain that I should never return the money.

I left Marseilles by myself, and after crossing the Alps arrived at Turin.

There I had a warm welcome from the Chevalier Raiberti and the Comte de la Perouse. Both of them pronounced me to be looking older, but I consoled myself with the thought that, after all, I was only forty-four.

I became an intimate friend of the English ambassador, Sir N——, a rich, accomplished and cultured man, who kept the choicest of tables. Everybody loved him, and amongst others this feeling was warmly shared by a Parmese girl, named Campioni, who was wonderfully beautiful.

As soon as I had told my friends that I intended to go into Switzerland to print at my own expense a refutation in Italian of the "History of the Venetian Government," by Amelot de la Houssaye, they all did their best by subscribing and obtaining subscriptions. The most generous of all was the Comte de la Perouse, who gave me two hundred and fifty francs for fifty copies. I left Turin in a week with two thousand lire in my purse. With this I should be able to print the book I had composed in my prison; but I should have to rewrite it 'ab initio', with the volume to my hand, as also the "History of Venice," by Nani.

When I had got these works I set out with the intention of having my book printed at Lugano, as there was a good press there and no censure. I also knew that the head of the press was a well-read man, and that the place abounded in good cheer and good society.

Lugano is near Milan, Como, and Lake Maggiore, and I was well pleased with the situation. I went to the best inn, which was kept by a man named Tagoretti, who gave me the best room in the house.

The day after my arrival I called on Dr. Agnelli, who was at once printer, priest, theologian, and an honest man. I made a regular agreement with him, he engaging to print at the rate of four sheets a week, and on my side I promised to pay him every week. He reserved the right of censorship, expressing a hope that our opinions might coincide.

I gave him the preface and the preliminary matter at once, and chose the paper and the size, large octavo.

When I got back to my inn the landlord told me that the bargello, or chief constable, wanted to see me.

Although Lugano is in Switzerland, its municipal government is modelled after that of the Italian towns.

I was curious to hear what this ill-omened personage could have to say to me, so I told him to shew him in. After giving me a profound bow, with his hat in his hand, Signor Bargello told me that he had come to offer me his services, and to assure me that I should enjoy complete tranquillity and safety in Lugano, whether from any enemies within the State or from the Venetian Government, in case I had any dispute with it.

"I thank you, signor," I replied, "and I am sure that you are telling me the truth, as I am in Switzerland."

"I must take the liberty of telling you, sir, that it is customary for strangers who take up their residence in Lugano, to pay some trifling sum, either by the week, the month, or the year."

"And if they refuse to pay?"

"Then their safety is not so sure."

"Money does everything in Lugano, I suppose."

"But, sir——"

"I understand, but let me tell you that I have no fears, and I shall consequently beg to be excused from paying anything."

"You will forgive me, but I happen to know that you have some disputes with the Venetian Government."

"You are making a mistake, my good fellow."

"No, I am not."

"If you are so sure, find someone to bet me two hundred sequins that I have reason to fear the Venetian Government; I will take the bet and deposit the amount."

The bargello remained silent, and the landlord told him he seemed to have made some kind of mistake, so he went away, looking very disappointed.

My landlord was delighted to hear that I thought of making some stay at Lugano, and advised me to call on the high bailiff, who governed the place.

"He's a very nice Swiss gentleman," said he, "and his wife a clever woman, and as fair as the day."

"I will go and see him to-morrow."

I sent in my name to the high bailiff at noon on the day following, and what was my surprise to find myself in the presence of M. de R and his charming wife. Beside her was a pretty boy, five or six years old.

Our mutual surprise may be imagined!

CHAPTER XI

The Punishment of Marazzani—I Leave Lugano—Turin—M. Dubois at Parma—Leghorn—The Duke of Orloff—Pisa—Stratico—Sienna—The Marchioness Chigi—My Departure from Sienna With an Englishwoman

These unforeseen, haphazard meetings with old friends have always been the happiest moments of my life.

We all remained for some time dumb with delight. M. de R. was the first to break the silence by giving me a cordial embrace. We burst out into mutual excuses, he for having imagined that there might be other Casanovas in Italy, and I for not having ascertained his name. He made me take pot-luck with him the same day, and we seemed as if we had never parted. The Republic had given him this employ—a very lucrative one—and he was only sorry that it would expire in two years. He told me he was delighted to be able to be of use to me, and begged me to consider he was wholly at my service. He was delighted to hear that I should be engaged in seeing my work through the press for three or four months, and seemed vexed when I told him that I could not accept his hospitality more than once a week as my labours would be incessant.

Madame de R—— could scarcely recover from her surprise. It was nine years since I had seen her at Soleure, and then I thought her beauty must be at its zenith; but I was wrong, she was still more beautiful and I told her so. She shewed me her only child, who had been born four years after my departure. She cherished the child as the apple of her eye, and seemed likely to spoil it; but I heard, a few years ago, that this child is now an amiable and accomplished man.

In a quarter of an hour Madame de R—— informed me of all that had happened at Soleure since my departure. Lebel had gone to Besancon, where he lived happily with his charming wife.

She happened to observe in a casual way that I no longer looked as young as I had done at Soleure, and this made me regulate my conduct in a manner I might not otherwise have done. I did not let her beauty carry me away; I resisted the effect of her charms, and I was content to enjoy her friendship, and to be worthy of the friendship of her good husband.

The work on which I was engaged demanded all my care and attention, and a love affair would have wasted most of my time.

I began work the next morning, and save for an hour's visit from M. de R—— I wrote on till nightfall. The next day I had the first proof-sheet with which I was well enough pleased.

I spent the whole of the next month in my room, working assiduously, and only going out to mass on feast days, to dine with M. de R——, and to walk with his wife and her child.

At the end of a month my first volume was printed and stitched, and the manuscript of the second volume was ready for the press. Towards the end of October the printer sent in the entire work in three volumes, and in less than a year the edition was sold out.

My object was not so much to make money as to appease the wrath of the Venetian Inquisitors; I had gone all over Europe, and experienced a violent desire to see my native land once more.

Amelot de la Houssaye had written his book from the point of view of an enemy of Venice. His history was rather a satire, containing learned and slanderous observations mingled together. It had been published for seventy years, but hitherto no one had taken the trouble to refute it. If a Venetian had attempted to do so he would not have obtained permission from his Government to print it in the States of Venice, for the State policy is to allow no one to discuss the actions of the authorities, whether in praise or blame; consequently no writer had attempted to refute the French history, as it was well known that the refutation would be visited with punishment and not with reward.

My position was an exceptional one. I had been persecuted by the Venetian Government, so no one could accuse me of being partial; and by my exposing the calumnies of Amelot before all Europe I hoped to gain a reward, which after all would only be an act of justice.

I had been an exile for fourteen years, and I thought the Inquisitors would be glad to repair their injustice on the pretext of rewarding my patriotism.

My readers will see that my hopes were fulfilled, but I had to wait for five more years instead of receiving permission to return at once.

M. de Bragadin was dead, and Dandolo and Barbaro were the only friends I had left at Venice; and with their aid I contrived to subscribe fifty copies of my book in my native town.

Throughout my stay at Lugano I only frequented the house of M. de R——, where I saw the Abbe Riva, a learned and discreet man, to whom I had been commended by M. Querini, his relation. The abbe enjoyed such a reputation for wisdom amongst his fellow-countrymen that he was a kind of arbiter in all disputes, and thus the expenses of the law were saved. It was no wonder that the gentlemen of the long robe hated him most cordially. His nephew, Jean Baptiste Riva, was a friend of the Muses, of Bacchus, and of Venus; he was also a friend of mine, though I could not match him with the bottles. He lent me all the nymphs he had initiated into the mysteries, and they liked him all the better, as I made them some small presents. With him and his two pretty sisters I went to the Borromean Isles. I knew that Count Borromeo, who had honoured me with his friendship at Turin, was there, and from him I felt certain of a warm welcome. One of the two sisters had to pass for Riva's wife, and the other for his sister-in-law.

Although the count was a ruined man he lived in his isles like a prince.

It would be impossible to describe these Islands of the Blest; they must be seen to be imagined. The inhabitants enjoy an everlasting spring; there is neither heat nor cold.

The count regaled us choicely, and amused the two girls by giving them rods and lines and letting them fish. Although he was ugly, old, and ruined, he still possessed the art of pleasing.

On the way back to Lugano, as I was making place for a carriage in a narrow road, my horse slipped and fell down a slope ten feet high. My head went against a large stone, and I thought my last hour was come as the blood poured out of the wound. However, I was well again in a few days. This was my last ride on horseback.

During my stay at Lugano the inspectors of the Swiss cantons came there in its turn. The people dignified them with the magnificent title of ambassadors, but M. de R—— was content to call them avoyers.

These gentlemen stayed at my inn, and I had my meals with them throughout their stay.

The avoyer of Berne gave me some news of my poor friend M. F——. His charming daughter Sara had become the wife of M. de V——, and was happy.

A few days after these pleasant and cultured men had left, I was startled one morning by the sudden appearance of the wretched Marazzani in my room. I seized him by his collar, threw him out, and before he had time to use his cane or his sword, I had kicked, beaten, and boxed him most soundly. He defended himself to the best of his ability, and the landlord and his men ran up at the noise, and had some difficulty in separating us.

"Don't let him go!" I cried, "send for the bargello and have him away to prison."

I dressed myself hastily, and as I was going out to see M. de R——, the bargello met me, and asked me on what charge I gave the man into custody.

"You will hear that at M. de R——'s, where I shall await you."

I must now explain my anger. You may remember, reader, that I left the wretched fellow in the prison of Buen Retiro. I heard afterwards that the King of Spain, Jerusalem, and the Canary Islands, had given him a small post in a galley off the coast of Africa.

He had done me no harm, and I pitied him; but not being his intimate friend, and having no power to mitigate the hardship of his lot, I had well-nigh forgotten him.

Eight months after, I met at Barcelona Madame Bellucci, a Venetian dancer, with whom I had had a small intrigue. She gave an exclamation of delight on seeing me, and said she was glad to see me delivered from the hard fate to which a tyrannous Government had condemned me.

"What fate is that?" I asked, "I have seen a good deal of misfortune since I left you."

"I mean the presidio."

"But that has never been my lot, thank God! Who told you such a story?"

"A Count Marazzani, who was here three weeks ago, and told me he had been luckier than you, as he had made his escape."

"He's a liar and a scoundrel; and if ever I meet him again he shall pay me dearly."

From that moment I never thought of the rascal without feeling a lively desire to give him a thrashing, but I never thought that chance would bring about so early a meeting.

Under the circumstances I think my behaviour will be thought only natural. I had beaten him, but that was not enough for me. I seemed to have done nothing, and indeed, I had got as good as I gave.

In the mean time he was in prison, and I went to M. de R—— to see what he could do for me.

As soon as M. de R heard my statement he said he could neither keep him in prison nor drive him out of the town unless I laid a plea before him, craving protection against this man, whom I believed to have come to Lugano with the purpose of assassinating me.

"You can make the document more effective," he added, "by placing your actual grievance in a strong light, and laying stress on his sudden appearance in your room without sending in his name. That's what you had better do, and it remains to be seen how I shall answer your plea. I shall ask him for his passport and delay the case, and order him to be severely treated; but in the end I shall only be able to drive him out of the town, unless he can find good bail."

I could ask no more. I sent in my plea, and the next day I had the pleasure of seeing him brought into the court bound hand and foot.

M. de R began to examine him, and Marazzani swore he had no evil intentions in calling on me. As to the calumny, he protested he had only repeated common rumour, and professed his joy at finding it had been mistaken.

This ought to have been enough for me, but I continued obdurate.

M. de R—— said the fact of my being sent to the galleys having been rumoured was no justification for his repeating it.

"And furthermore," he proceeded, "M. Casanova's suspicion that you were going to assassinate him is justified by your giving a false name, for the plaintiff maintains that you are not Count Marazzani at all. He offers to furnish surety on this behalf, and if M. Casanova does you wrong, his bail will escheat to you as damages. In the mean time you will remain in prison till we have further information about your real status."

He was taken back, and as the poor devil had not a penny in his pocket it would have been superfluous to tell the bargedlo to treat him severely.

M. de R wrote to the Swiss agent at Parma to obtain the necessary information; but as the rascal knew this would be against him, he wrote me a humble letter, in which he confessed that he was the son of a poor shopkeeper of Bobbio, and although his name was really Marazzani, he had nothing to do with the Marazzanis of Plaisance. He begged me to set him at liberty.

I shewed the letter to M. de R——, who let him out of prison with orders to leave Lugano in twenty-four hours.

I thought I had been rather too harsh with him, and gave the poor devil some money to take him to Augsburg, and also a letter for M. de Sellentin, who was recruiting there for the Prussian king. We shall hear of Marazzani again.

The Chevalier de Breche came to the Lugano Fair to buy some horses, and stopped a fortnight. I often met him at M. de R——'s, for whose wife he had a great admiration, and I was sorry to see him go.

I left Lugano myself a few days later, having made up my mind to winter in Turin, where I hoped to see some pleasant society.

Before I left I received a friendly letter from Prince Lubomirski, with a bill for a hundred ducats, in payment of fifty copies of my book. The prince had become lord high marshal on the death of Count Bilinski.

When I got to Turin I found a letter from the noble Venetian M. Girolamo Zulian, the same that had given me an introduction to Mocenigo. His letter contained an enclosure to M. Berlendis, the representative of the Republic at Turin, who thanked me for having enabled him to receive me.

The ambassador, a rich man, and a great lover of the fair sex, kept up a splendid establishment, and this was enough for his Government, for intelligence is not considered a necessary qualification for a Venetian ambassador. Indeed it is a positive disadvantage, and a witty ambassador would no doubt fall into disgrace with the Venetian Senate. However, Berlendis ran no risk whatever on this score; the realm of wit was an unknown land to him.

I got this ambassador to call the attention of his Government to the work I had recently published, and the answer the State Inquisitors gave may astonish my readers, but it did not astonish me. The secretary of the famous and accursed Tribunal wrote to say that he had done well to call the attention of the Inquisitors to this work, as the author's presumption appeared on the title-page. He added that the work would be examined, and in the mean time the ambassador was instructed to shew me no signal marks of favour lest the Court should suppose he was protecting me as a Venetian.

Nevertheless, it was the same tribunal that had facilitated my access to the ambassador to Madrid—Mocenigo.

I told Berlendis that my visits should be limited in number, and free from all ostentation.

I was much interested in his son's tutor; he was a priest, a man of letters, and a poet. His name was Andreis, and he is now resident in England, where he enjoys full liberty, the greatest of all blessings.

I spent my time at Turin very pleasantly, in the midst of a small circle of Epicureans; there were the old Chevalier Raiberti, the Comte de la Perouse, a certain Abbe Roubien, a delightful man, the voluptuous Comte de Riva, and the English ambassador. To the amusements which this society afforded I added a course of reading, but no love affairs whatever.

While I was at Turin, a milliner, Perouse's mistress, feeling herself in 'articulo mortis', swallowed the portrait of her lover instead of the Eucharist. This incident made me compose two sonnets, which pleased me a good deal at the time, and with which I am still satisfied. No doubt some will say that every poet is pleased with his own handiwork, but as a matter of fact, the severest critic of a sensible author is himself.

The Russian squadron, under the command of Count Alexis Orloff, was then at Leghorn; this squadron threatened Constantinople, and would probably have taken it if an Englishman had been in command.

As I had known Count Orloff in Russia, I imagined that I might possibly render myself of service to him, and at the same time make my fortune.

The English ambassador having given me a letter for the English consul, I left Turin with very little money in my purse and no letter of credit on any banker.

An Englishman named Acton commended me to an English banker at Leghorn, but this letter did not empower me to draw any supplies.

Acton was just then involved in a curious complication. When he was at Venice he had fallen in love with a pretty woman, either a Greek or a Neapolitan. The husband, by birth a native of Turin, and by profession a good-for-nothing, placed no obstacle in Acton's way, as the Englishman was generous with his money; but he had a knack of turning up at those moments when his absence would have been most desirable.

The generous but proud and impatient Englishman could not be expected to bear this for long. He consulted with the lady, and determined to shew his teeth. The husband persisted in his untimely visits, and one day Acton said, dryly,—

"Do you want a thousand guineas? You can have them if you like, on the condition that your wife travels with me for three years without our having the pleasure of your society."

The husband thought the bargain a good one, and signed an agreement to that effect.

After the three years were over the husband wrote to his wife, who was   at Venice, to return to him, and to Acton to put no obstacle in the way.

The lady replied that she did not want to live with him any more, and Acton explained to the husband that he could not be expected to drive his mistress away against her will. He foresaw, however, that the husband would complain to the English ambassador, and determined to be before-handed with him.

In due course the husband did apply to the English ambassador, requesting him to compel Acton to restore to him his lawful wife. He even asked the Chevalier Raiberti to write to the Commendatore Camarana, the Sardinian ambassador at Venice, to apply pressure on the Venetian Government, and he would doubtless have succeeded if M. Raiberti had done him this favour. However, as it was he did nothing of the sort, and even gave Acton a warm welcome when he came to Turin to look into the matter. He had left his mistress at Venice under the protection of the English consul.

The husband was ashamed to complain publicly, as he would have been confronted with the disgraceful agreement he had signed; but Berlendis maintained that he was in the right, and argued the question in the most amusing manner. On the one hand he urged the sacred and inviolable character of the marriage rite, and on the other he shewed how the wife was bound to submit to her husband in all things. I argued the matter with him myself, shewing him his disgraceful position in defending a man who traded on his wife's charms, and he was obliged to give in when I assured him that the husband had offered to renew the lease for the same time and on the same terms as before.

Two years later I met Acton at Bologna, and admired the beauty whom he considered and treated as his wife. She held on her knees a fine little Acton.

I left Turin for Parma with a Venetian who, like myself, was an exile from his country. He had turned actor to gain a livelihood; and was going to Parma with two actresses, one of whom was interesting. As soon as I found out who he was, we became friends, and he would have gladly made me a partner in all his amusements, by the way, if I had been in the humour to join him.

This journey to Leghorn was undertaken under the influence of chimerical ideas. I thought I might be useful to Count Orloff, in the conquest he was going to make, as it was said, of Constantinople. I fancied that it had been decreed by fate that without me he could never pass through the Dardanelles. In spite of the wild ideas with which my mind was occupied, I conceived a warm friendship for my travelling companion, whose name was Angelo Bentivoglio. The Government never forgave him a certain crime, which to the philosophic eye appears a mere trifle. In four years later, when I describe my stay at Venice, I shall give some further account of him.

About noon we reached Parma, and I bade adieu to Bentivoglio and his friends. The Court was at Colorno, but having nothing to gain from this mockery of a court, and wishing to leave for Bologna the next morning, I asked Dubois-Chateleraux, Chief of the Mint, and a talented though vain man, to give me some dinner. The reader will remember that I had known him twenty two years before, when I was in love with Henriette. He was delighted to see me, and seemed to set great store by my politeness in giving him the benefit of my short stay at Parma. I told him that Count Orloff was waiting for me at Leghorn, and that I was obliged to travel day and night.

"He will be setting sail before long," said he; "I have advices from Leghorn to that effect."

I said in a mysterious tone of voice that he would not sail without me, and I could see that my host treated me with increased respect after this. He wanted to discuss the Russian Expedition, but my air of reserve made him change the conversation.

At dinner we talked a good deal about Henriette, whom he said he had succeeded in finding out; but though he spoke of her with great respect, I took care not to give him any information on the subject. He spent the whole afternoon in uttering complaints against the sovereigns of Europe, the King of Prussia excepted, as he had made him a baron, though I never could make out why.

He cursed the Duke of Parma who persisted in retaining his services, although there was no mint in existence in the duchy, and his talents were consequently wasted there.

I listened to all his complaints, and agreed that Louis XV. had been ungrateful in not conferring the Order of St. Michael on him; that Venice had rewarded his services very shabbily; that Spain was stingy, and Naples devoid of honesty, etc., etc. When he had finished, I asked him if he could give me a bill on a banker for fifty sequins.

He replied in the most friendly manner that he would not give me the trouble of going to a banker for such a wretched sum as that; he would be delighted to oblige me himself.

I took the money promising to repay him at an early date, but I have never been able to do so. I do not know whether he is alive or dead, but if he were to attain the age of Methuselah I should not entertain any hopes of paying him; for I get poorer every day, and feel that my end is not far off.

The next day I was in Bologna, and the day after in Florence, where I met the Chevalier Morosini, nephew of the Venetian procurator, a young man of nineteen, who was travelling with Count Stratico, professor of mathematics at the University of Padua. He gave me a letter for his brother, a Jacobin monk, and professor of literature at Pisa, where I stopped for a couple of hours on purpose to make the celebrated monk's acquaintance. I found him even greater than his fame, and promised to come again to Pisa, and make a longer stay for the purpose of enjoying his society.

I stopped an hour at the Wells, where I made the acquaintance of the
Pretender to the throne of Great Britain, and from there went on to Leghorn, where I found Count Orloff still waiting, but only because
contrary winds kept him from sailing.

The English consul, with whom he was staying, introduced me at once to the Russian admiral, who received me with expressions of delight. He told me he would be charmed if I would come on board with him. He told me to have my luggage taken off at once, as he would set sail with the first fair wind. When he was gone the English consul asked me what would be my status with the admiral.

"That's just what I mean to find out before embarking my effects."

"You won't be able to speak to him till to-morrow." Next morning I called on Count Orloff, and sent him in a short note, asking him to give me a short interview before I embarked my mails.

An officer came out to tell me that the admiral was writing in bed, and hoped I would wait.

"Certainly."

I had been waiting a few minutes, when Da Loglio, the Polish agent at Venice and an old friend of mine, came in. "What are you doing here, my dear Casanova?" said he.

"I am waiting for an interview with the admiral."

"He is very busy."

After this, Da Loglio coolly went into the admiral's room. This was impertinent of him; it was as if he said in so many words that the admiral was too busy to see me, but not too busy to see him.

A moment after, Marquis Manucci came in with his order of St. Anne and his formal air. He congratulated me on my visit to Leghorn, and then said he had read my work on Venice, and had been surprised to find himself in it.

He had some reason for surprise, for there was no connection between him and the subject-matter; but he should have discovered before that the unexpected often happens. He did not give me time to tell him so, but went into the admiral's room as Da Loglio had done.

I was vexed to see how these gentlemen were admitted while I danced attendance, and the project of sailing with Orloff began to displease me.

In five hours Orloff came out followed by a numerous train. He told me pleasantly that we could have our talk at table or after dinner.

"After dinner, if you please," I said.

He came in and sat down at two o'clock, and I was among the guests.

Orloff kept on saying, "Eat away, gentlemen, eat away;" and read his correspondence and gave his secretary letters all the time.

After dinner he suddenly glanced up at me, and taking me by the hand led me to the window, and told me to make haste with my luggage, as he should sail before the morning if the wind kept up.

"Quite so; but kindly tell me, count, what is to be my status or employment an board your ship?"

"At present I have no special employ to give you; that will come in time.
Come on board as my friend."

"The offer is an honourable one so far as you are concerned, but all the other officers might treat me with contempt. I should be regarded as a kind of fool, and I should probably kill the first man who dared to insult me. Give me a distinct office, and let me wear your uniform; I will be useful to you. I know the country for which you are bound, I can speak the language, and I am not wanting in courage."

"My dear sir, I really have no particular office to give you."

"Then, count, I wish you a pleasant sail; I am going to Rome. I hope you may never repent of not taking me, for without me you will never pass the Dardanelles."

"Is that a prophecy?"

"It's an oracle."

"We will test its veracity, my dear Calchus."

Such was the short dialogue I had with the worthy count, who, as a matter of fact, did not pass the Dardanelles. Whether he would have succeeded if I had been on board is more than I can say.

Next day I delivered my letters to M. Rivarola and the English banker.
The squadron had sailed in the early morning.

The day after I went to Pisa, and spent a pleasant week in the company of Father Stratico, who was made a bishop two or three years after by means of a bold stroke that might have ruined him. He delivered a funeral oration over Father Ricci, the last general of the Jesuits. The Pope, Ganganelli, had the choice of punishing the writer and increasing the odium of many of the faithful, or of rewarding him handsomely. The sovereign pontiff followed the latter course. I saw the bishop some years later, and he told me in confidence that he had only written the oration because he felt certain, from his knowledge of the human heart, that his punishment would be a great reward.

This clever monk initiated me into all the charms of Pisan society. He had organized a little choir of ladies of rank, remarkable for their intelligence and beauty, and had taught them to sing extempore to the guitar. He had had them instructed by the famous Gorilla, who was crowned poetess-laureate at the capitol by night, six years later. She was crowned where our great Italian poets were crowned; and though her merit was no doubt great, it was, nevertheless, more tinsel than gold, and not of that order to place her on a par with Petrarch or Tasso.

She was satirised most bitterly after she had received the bays; and the satirists were even more in the wrong than the profaners of the capitol, for all the pamphlets against her laid stress on the circumstance that chastity, at all events, was not one of her merits. All poetesses, from the days of Homer to our own, have sacrificed on the altar of Venus. No one would have heard of Gorilla if she had not had the sense to choose her lovers from the ranks of literary men; and she would never have been crowned at Rome if she had not succeeded in gaining over Prince Gonzaga Solferino, who married the pretty Mdlle. Rangoni, daughter of the Roman consul, whom I knew at Marseilles, and of whom I have already spoken.

This coronation of Gorilla is a blot on the pontificate of the present Pope, for henceforth no man of genuine merit will accept the honour which was once so carefully guarded by the giants of human intellect.

Two days after the coronation Gorilla and her admirers left Rome, ashamed of what they had done. The Abbe Pizzi, who had been the chief promoter of her apotheosis, was so inundated with pamphlets and satires that for some months he dared not shew his face.

This is a long digression, and I will now return to Father Stratico, who made the time pass so pleasantly for me.

Though he was not a handsome man, he possessed the art of persuasion to perfection; and he succeeded in inducing me to go to Sienna, where he said I should enjoy myself. He gave me a letter of introduction for the Marchioness Chigi, and also one for the Abbe Chiaccheri; and as I had nothing better to do I went to Sienna by the shortest way, not caring to visit Florence.

The Abbe Chiaccheri gave me a warm welcome, and promised to do all he could to amuse me; and he kept his word. He introduced me himself to the Marchioness Chigi, who took me by storm as soon as she had read the letter of the Abbe Stratico, her dear abbe, as she called him, when she read the superscription in his writing.

The marchioness was still handsome, though her beauty had begun to wane; but with her the sweetness, the grace, and the ease of manner supplied the lack of youth. She knew how to make a compliment of the slightest expression, and was totally devoid of any affection of superiority.

"Sit down," she began. "So you are going to stay a week, I see, from the dear abbe's letter. That's a short time for us, but perhaps it may be too long for you. I hope the abbe has not painted us in too rosy colours."

"He only told me that I was to spend a week here, and that I should find with you all the charms of intellect and sensibility."

"Stratico should have condemned you to a month without mercy."

"Why mercy? What hazard do I run?"

"Of being tired to death, or of leaving some small morsel of your heart at Sienna."

"All that might happen in a week, but I am ready to dare the danger, for Stratico has guarded me from the first by counting on you, and from the second by counting on myself. You will receive my pure and intelligent homage. My heart will go forth from Sienna as free as it came, for I have no hope of victory, and defeat would make me wretched."

"Is it possible that you are amongst the despairing?"

"Yes, and to that fact I owe my happiness."

"It would be a pity for you if you found yourself mistaken."

"Not such a pity as you may think, Madam. 'Carpe diem' is my motto. 'Tis likewise the motto of that finished voluptuary, Horace, but I only take it because it suits me. The pleasure which follows desires is the best, for it is the most acute.

"True, but it cannot be calculated on, and defies the philosopher. May God preserve you, madam, from finding out this painful truth by experience! The highest good lies in enjoyment; desire too often remains unsatisfied. If you have not yet found out the truth of Horace's maxim, I congratulate you."

The amiable marchioness smiled pleasantly and gave no positive answer.

Chiaccheri now opened his mouth for the first time, and said that the greatest happiness he could wish us was that we should never agree. The marchioness assented, rewarding Chiaccheri with a smile, but I could not do so.

"I had rather contradict you," I said, "than renounce all hopes of pleasing you. The abbe has thrown the apple of discord between us, but if we continue as we have begun I shall take up my abode at Sienna."

The marchioness was satisfied with the sample of her wit which she had given me, and began to talk commonplaces, asking me if I should like to see company and enjoy society of the fair sex. She promised to take me everywhere.

"Pray do not take the trouble," I replied. "I want to leave Sienna with the feeling that you are the only lady to whom I have done homage, and that the Abbe Chiaccheri has been my only guide."

The marchioness was flattered, and asked the abbe and myself to dine with her on the following day in a delightful house she had at a hundred paces from the town.

The older I grew the more I became attached to the intellectual charms of women. With the sensualist, the contrary takes place; he becomes more material in his old age: requires women well taught in Venus's shrines, and flies from all mention of philosophy.

As I was leaving her I told the abbe that if I stayed at Sienna I would see no other woman but her, come what might, and he agreed that I was very right.

The abbe shewed me all the objects of interest in Sienna, and introduced me to the literati, who in their turn visited me.

The same day Chiaccheri took me to a house where the learned society assembled. It was the residence of two sisters—the elder extremely ugly and the younger very pretty, but the elder sister was accounted, and very rightly, the Corinna of the place. She asked me to give her a specimen of my skill, promising to return the compliment. I recited the first thing that came into my head, and she replied with a few lines of exquisite beauty. I complimented her, but Chiaccheri (who had been her master) guessed that I did not believe her to be the author, and proposed that we should try bouts rimes. The pretty sister gave out the rhymes, and we all set to work. The ugly sister finished first, and when the verses came to be read, hers were pronounced the best. I was amazed, and made an improvisation on her skill, which I gave her in writing. In five minutes she returned it to me; the rhymes were the same, but the turn of the thought was much more elegant. I was still more surprised, and took the liberty of asking her name, and found her to be the famous "Shepherdess," Maria Fortuna, of the Academy of Arcadians.

I had read the beautiful stanzas she had written in praise of Metastasio.
I told her so, and she brought me the poet's reply in manuscript.

Full of admiration, I addressed myself to her alone, and all her plainness vanished.

I had had an agreeable conversation with the marchioness in the morning, but in the evening I was literally in an ecstacy.

I kept on talking of Fortuna, and asked the abbe if she could improvise in the manner of Gorilla. He replied that she had wished to do so, but that he had disallowed it, and he easily convinced me that this improvisation would have been the ruin of her fine talent. I also agreed with him when he said that he had warned her against making impromptus too frequently, as such hasty verses are apt to sacrifice wit to rhyme.

The honour in which improvisation was held amongst the Greeks and Romans is due to the fact that Greek and Latin verse is not under the dominion of rhyme. But as it was, the great poets seldom improvised; knowing as they did that such verses were usually feeble and common-place.

Horace often passed a whole night searching for a vigorous and elegantly-turned phrase. When he had succeeded, he wrote the words on the wall and went to sleep. The lines which cost him nothing are generally prosaic; they may easily be picked out in his epistles.

The amiable and learned Abbe Chiaccheri, confessed to me that he was in love with his pupil, despite her ugliness. He added that he had never expected it when he began to teach her to make verses.

"I can't understand that," I said, "sublata lucerna', you know."

"Not at all," said he, with a laugh, "I love her for her face, since it is inseparable from my idea of her."

A Tuscan has certainly more poetic riches at his disposal than any other Italian, and the Siennese dialect is sweeter and more energetic than that of Florence, though the latter claims the title of the classic dialect, on account of its purity. This purity, together with its richness and copiousness of diction it owes to the academy. From the great richness of Italian we can treat a subject with far greater eloquence than a French writer; Italian abounds in synonyms, while French is lamentably deficient in this respect. Voltaire used to laugh at those who said that the French tongue could not be charged with poverty, as it had all that was necessary. A man may have necessaries, and yet be poor. The obstinacy of the French academy in refusing to adopt foreign words skews more pride than wisdom. This exclusiveness cannot last.

As for us we take words from all languages and all sources, provided they suit the genius of our own language. We love to see our riches increase; we even steal from the poor, but to do so is the general characteristic of the rich.

The amiable marchioness gave us a delicious dinner in a house designed   by
Palladio. Chiaccheri had warned me to say nothing about the Shepherdess
Fortuna; but at dinner she told him she was sure he had taken me to   her
house. He had not the face to deny it, and I did not conceal the pleasure
I had received.

"Stratico admires Fortuna," said the marchioness, "and I confess that her writings have great merit, but it's a pity one cannot go to the house, except under an incognito."

"Why not?" I asked, in some astonishment.

"What!" said she to the abbe, "you did not tell him whose house it is?"

"I did not think it necessary, her father and mother rarely shew themselves."

"Well, it's of no consequence."

"But what is her father?" I asked, "the hangman, perhaps?"

"Worse, he's the 'bargello', and you must see that a stranger cannot be received into good society here if he goes to such places as that."

Chiaccheri looked rather hurt, and I thought it my duty to say that I would not go there again till the eve of my departure.

"I saw her sister once," said the marchioness; "she is really charmingly pretty, and it's a great pity that with her beauty and irreproachable morality she should be condemned to marry a man of her father's class."

"I once knew a man named Coltellini," I replied; "he is the son of the bargello of Florence, and is poet-in-ordinary to the Empress of Russia. I shall try to make a match between him and Fortuna's sister; he is a young man of the greatest talents."

The marchioness thought my idea an excellent one, but soon after I heard that Coltellini was dead.

The 'bargello' is a cordially-detested person all over Italy, if you except Modena, where the weak nobility make much of the 'bargello', and do justice to his excellent table. This is a curious fact, for as a rule these bargellos are spies, liars, traitors, cheats, and misanthropes, for a man despised hates his despisers.

At Sienna I was shewn a Count Piccolomini, a learned and agreeable man. He had a strange whim, however, of spending six months in the year in the strictest seclusion in his own house, never going out and never seeing any company; reading and working the whole time. He certainly did his best to make up for his hibernation during the other six months in the year.

The marchioness promised she would come to Rome in the course of the summer. She had there an intimate friend in Bianconi who had abandoned the practice of medicine, and was now the representative of the Court of Saxony.

On the eve of my departure, the driver who was to take me to Rome came and asked me if I would like to take a travelling companion, and save myself three sequins.

"I don't want anyone."

"You are wrong, for she is very beautiful."

"Is she by herself?"

"No, she is with a gentleman on horseback, who wishes to ride all the way to Rome."

"Then how did the girl come here?"

"On horseback, but she is tired out, and cannot bear it any longer. The gentleman has offered me four sequins to take her to Rome, and as I am a poor man I think you might let me earn the money."

"I suppose he will follow the carriage?"

"He can go as he likes; that can't make much difference to either of us."

"You say she is young and pretty."

"I have been told so, but I haven't seen her myself."

"What sort of a man is her companion?"

"He's a fine man, but he can speak very little Italian."

"Has he sold the lady's horse?"

"No, it was hired. He has only one trunk, which will go behind the carriage."

"This is all very strange. I shall not give any decision before speaking to this man."

"I will tell him to wait on you."

Directly afterwards, a brisk-looking young fellow, carrying himself well enough, and clad in a fancy uniform, came in. He told me the tale I had heard from the coachman, and ended by saying that he was sure I would not refuse to accommodate his wife in my carriage.

"Your wife, sir?"

I saw he was a Frenchman, and I addressed him in French.

"God be praised! You can speak my native tongue. Yes, sir, she is an Englishwoman and my wife. I am sure she will be no trouble to you."

"Very good. I don't want to start later than I had arranged. Will she be ready at five o'clock?"

"Certainly."

The next morning when I got into my carriage, I found her already there. I paid her some slight compliment, and sat down beside her, and we drove off.

CHAPTER XII

Miss Betty—The Comte de L'Etoile—Sir B * * * M * * *—
Reassured

This was the fourth adventure I had had of this kind. There is nothing particularly out of the common in having a fellow-traveller in one's carriage; this time, however, the affair had something decidedly romantic about it.

I was forty-five, and my purse contained two hundred sequins. I still loved the fair sex, though my ardour had decreased, my experience had ripened, and my caution increased. I was more like a heavy father than a young lover, and I limited myself to pretensions of the most modest character.

The young person beside me was pretty and gentle-looking, she was neatly though simply dressed in the English fashion, she was fair and small, and her budding breast could be seen outlined beneath the fine muslin of her dress. She had all the appearances of modesty and noble birth, and something of virginal innocence, which inspired one with attachment and respect at the same time.

"I hope you can speak French madam?" I began.

"Yes, and a little Italian too."

"I congratulate myself on having you for my travelling companion."

"I think you should congratulate me."

"I heard you came to Sienna on horseback."

"Yes, but I will never do such a foolish thing again."

"I think your husband would have been wise to sell his horse and buy a carriage."

"He hired it; it does not belong to him. From Rome we are going to drive to Naples."

"You like travelling?"

"Very much, but with greater comfort."

With these words the English girl, whose white skin did not look as if it could contain a drop of blood, blushed most violently.

I guessed something of her secret, and begged pardon; and for more than an hour I remain silent, pretending to gaze at the scenery, but in reality thinking of her, for she began to inspire me with a lively interest.

Though the position of my young companion was more than equivocal, I determined to see my way clearly before I took any decisive step; and I waited patiently till we got to Bon Couvent, where we expected to dine and meet the husband.

We got there at ten o'clock.

In Italy the carriages never go faster than a walk; a man on foot can outstrip them, as they rarely exceed three miles an hour. The tedium of a journey under such circumstances is something dreadful, and in the hot months one has to stop five or six hours in the middle of the day to avoid falling ill.

My coachman said he did not want to go beyond St. Quirico, where there was an excellent inn, that night, so he proposed waiting at Bon Couvent till four o'clock. We had therefore six hours wherein to rest.

The English girl was astonished at not finding her husband, and looked for him in all directions. I noticed her, and asked the landlord what had become of him. He informed us that he had breakfasted and baited his horse, and had then gone on, leaving word that he would await us at St. Quirico and order supper there.

I thought it all very strange, but I said nothing. The poor girl begged me to excuse her husband's behaviour.

"He has given me a mark of his confidence, madam, and there is nothing to be offended at."

The landlord asked me if the vetturino paid my expenses, and I answered in the negative; and the girl then told him to ask the vetturino if he was paying for her.

The man came in, and to convince the lady that providing her with meals was not in the contract, he gave her a paper which she handed to me to read. It was signed "Comte de l'Etoile."

When she was alone with me my young companion begged me only to order dinner for myself.

I understood her delicacy, and this made her all the dearer to me.

"Madame," said I, "you must please look upon me as an old friend. I guess you have no money about you, and that you wish to fast from motives of delicacy. Your husband shall repay me, if he will have it so. If I told the landlord to only prepare dinner for myself I should be dishonouring the count, yourself possibly, and myself most of all."

"I feel you are right sir. Let dinner be served for two, then; but I cannot eat, for I feel ill, and I hope you will not mind my lying on the bed for a moment."

"Pray do not let me disturb you. This is a pleasant room, and they can lay the table in the next. Lie down, and sleep if you can, and I will order dinner to be ready by two. I hope you will be feeling better by then."

I left her without giving her time to answer, and went to order dinner.

I had ceased to believe the Frenchman to be the beautiful Englishwoman's husband, and began to think I should have to fight him.

The case, I felt certain, was one of elopement and seduction; and, superstitious as usual, I was sure that my good genius had sent me in the nick of time to save her and care for her, and in short to snatch her from the hands of her infamous deceiver.

Thus I fondled my growing passion.

I laughed at the absurd title the rascal had given himself, and when the thought struck me that he had possibly abandoned her to me altogether, I made up my mind that he deserved hanging. Nevertheless, I resolved never to leave her.

I lay down on the bed, and as I built a thousand castles in the air I fell asleep.

The landlady awoke me softly, saying that three o'clock had struck.

"Wait a moment before you bring in the dinner. I will go and see if the lady is awake."

I opened the door gently, and saw she was still asleep, but as I closed the door after me the noise awoke her, and she asked if I had dined.

"I shall not take any dinner, madam, unless you do me the honour to dine with me. You have had a five hours' rest, and I hope you are better."

"I will sit down with you to dinner, as you wish it."

"That makes me happy, and I will order dinner to be served forthwith."

She ate little, but what little she did eat was taken with a good appetite. She was agreeably surprised to see the beefsteaks and plum pudding, which I had ordered for her.

When the landlady came in, she asked her if the cook was an Englishman, and when she heard that I had given directions for the preparation of her national dishes, she seemed full of gratitude.

She cheered up, and congratulated me on my appetite, while I encouraged her to drink some excellent Montepulciano and Montefiascone. By dessert she was in good spirits, while I felt rather excited. She told me, in Italian, that she was born in London, and I thought I should have died with joy, in reply to my question whether she knew Madame Cornelis, she replied that she had known her daughter as they had been at school together.

"Has Sophie grown tall?"

"No, she is quite small, but she is very pretty, and so clever."

"She must now be seventeen."

"Exactly. We are of the same age."

As she said this she blushed and lowered her eyes.

"Are you ill?"

"Not at all. I scarcely like to say it, but Sophie is the very image of you."

"Why should you hesitate to say so? It has been remarked to me before. No doubt it is a mere coincidence. How long ago is it since you have seen her?"

"Eighteen months; she went back to her mother's, to be married as it was said, but I don't know to whom."

"Your news interests me deeply."

The landlord brought me the bill, and I saw a note of three pains which her husband had spent on himself and his horse.

"He said you would pay," observed the landlord.

The Englishwoman blushed. I paid the bill, and we went on.

I was delighted to see her blushing, it proved she was not a party to her husband's proceedings.

I was burning with the desire to know how she had left London and had met the Frenchman, and why they were going to Rome; but I did not want to trouble her by my questions, and I loved her too well already to give her any pain.

We had a three hours' drive before us, so I turned the conversation to
Sophie, with whom she had been at school.

"Was Miss Nancy Steyne there when you left?" said I.

The reader may remember how fond I had been of this young lady, who had dined with me, and whom I had covered with kisses, though she was only twelve.

My companion sighed at hearing the name of Nancy, and told me that she had left.

"Was she pretty when you knew her?"

"She was a beauty, but her loveliness was a fatal gift to her. Nancy was a close friend of mine, we loved each other tenderly; and perhaps our sympathy arose from the similarity of the fate in store for us. Nancy, too loving and too simple, is now, perhaps, even more unhappy than myself."

"More unhappy? What do you mean?"

"Alas!"

"Is it possible that fate has treated you harshly? Is it possible that you can be unhappy with such a letter of commendation as nature has given you?"

"Alas! let us speak of something else."

Her countenance was suffused with emotion. I pitied her in secret, and led the conversation back to Nancy.

"Tell me why you think Nancy is unhappy."

"She ran away with a young man she loved; they despaired of gaining the parents' consent to the match. Since her flight nothing has been heard of her, and you see I have some reason to fear that she is unhappy."

"You are right. I would willingly give my life if it could be the saving of her."

"Where did you know her?"

"In my own house. She and Sophie dined with me, and her father came in at the end of the meal."

"Now I know who you are. How often have I heard Sophie talking of   you.

Nancy loved you as well as her father. I heard that you had gone to

Russia, and had fought a duel with a general in Poland. Is this true?   How I wish I could tell dear Sophie all this, but I may not entertain such

hopes now."

"You have heard the truth about me; but what should prevent you writing what you like to England? I take a lively interest in you, trust in me, and I promise you that you shall communicate with whom you please."

"I am vastly obliged to you."

With these words she became silent, and I left her to her thoughts.

At seven o'clock we arrived at St. Quirico, and the so-called Comte de l'Etoile came out and welcomed his wife in the most loving fashion, kissing her before everybody, no doubt with the object of giving people to understand that she was his wife, and I her father.

The girl responded to all his caresses, looking as if a load had been lifted off her breast, and without a word of reproach she went upstairs with him, having apparently forgotten my existence. I set that down to love, youth, and the forgetfulness natural to that early age.

I went upstairs in my turn with my carpet bag, and supper was served directly, as we had to start very early the next morning if we wished to reach Radicofani before the noonday heat.

We had an excellent supper, as the count had preceded us by six hours, and the landlord had had plenty of time to make his preparations. The English girl seemed as much in love with de l'Etoile as he with her, and I was left completely out in the cold. I cannot describe the high spirits, the somewhat risky sallies, and the outrageous humours of the young gentleman; the girl laughed with all her heart, and I could not help laughing too.

I considered that I was present at a kind of comedy, and not a gesture, not a word, not a laugh did I allow to escape me.

"He may be merely a rich and feather-brained young officer," I said to myself, "who treats everything in this farcical manner. He won't be the first of the species I have seen. They are amusing, but frivolous, and sometimes dangerous, wearing their honour lightly, and too apt to carry it at the sword's point."

On this hypothesis I was ill pleased with my position. I did not much like his manner towards myself; he seemed to be making a dupe of me, and behaved all the while as if he were doing me an honour.

On the supposition that the Englishwoman was his wife, his treatment of myself was certainly not warranted, and I was not the man to play zero. I could not disguise the fact, however, that any onlooker would have pronounced me to be playing an inferior part.

There were two beds in the room where we had our supper. When the chambermaid came to put on the sheets, I told her to give me another room. The count politely begged me to sleep in the same room with them, and the lady remained neutral; but I did not much care for their company, and insisted on leaving them alone.

I had my carpet bag taken to my room, wished them a good night and locked myself in. My friends had only one small trunk, whence I concluded that they had sent on their luggage by another way; but they did not even have the trunk brought up to their room. I went to bed tranquilly, feeling much less interested about the lady than I had been on the journey.

I was roused early in the morning, and made a hasty toilette. I could hear my neighbours dressing, so I half opened my door, and wished them good day without going into their room.

In a quarter of an hour I heard the sound of a dispute in the court-yard, and on looking out, there were the Frenchman and the vetturino arguing hotly. The vetturino held the horse's bridle, and the pretended count did his best to snatch it away from him.

I guessed the bone of contention: the Frenchman had no money, and the vetturino asked in vain for his due. I knew that I should be drawn into the dispute, and was making up my mind to do my duty without mercy, when the Count de l'Etoile came in and said,—

"This blockhead does not understand what I say to him; but as he may have right on his side, I must ask you to give him two sequins. I will return you the money at Rome. By an odd chance I happen to have no money about me, but the fellow might trust me as he has got my trunk. However, he says he must be paid, so will you kindly oblige me? You shall hear more of me at Rome."

Without waiting for me to reply, the rascal went out and ran down the stairs. The vetturino remained in the room. I put my head out of the window, and saw him leap on horseback and gallop away.

I sat down on my bed, and turned the scene over in my mind, rubbing my hands gently. At last I went off into a mad roar of laughter; it struck me as so whimsical and original an adventure.

"Laugh too," said I to the lady, "laugh or I will never get up."

"I agree with you that it's laughable enough, but I have not the spirit to laugh."

"Well, sit down at all events."

I gave the poor devil of a vetturino two sequins, telling him that I should like some coffee and to start in a quarter of an hour.

I was grieved to see my companion's sadness.

"I understand your grief," said I, "but you must try to overcome it. I have only one favour to ask of you, and if you refuse to grant me that, I shall be as sad as you, so we shall be rather a melancholy couple."

"What can I do for you?"

"You can tell me on your word of honour whether that extraordinary character is your husband, or only your lover."

"I will tell you the simple truth; he is not my husband, but we are going to be married at Rome."

"I breathe again. He never shall be your husband, and so much the better for you. He has seduced you, and you love him, but you will soon get over that."

"Never, unless he deceives me."

"He has deceived you already. I am sure he has told you that he is rich, that he is a man of rank, and that he will make you happy; and all that is a lie."

"How can you know all this?"

"Experience—experience is my great teacher. Your lover is a young feather-brain, a man of no worth. He might possibly marry you, but it would be only to support himself by the sale of your charms."

"He loves me; I am sure of it."

"Yes, he loves you, but not with the love of a man of honour. Without knowing my name, or my character, or anything about me, he delivered you over to my tender mercies. A man of any delicacy would never abandon his loved one thus."

"He is not jealous. You know Frenchmen are not."

"A man of honour is the same in France, and England, and Italy, and all the world over. If he loved you, would he have left you penniless in this fashion? What would you do, if I were inclined to play the brutal lover? You may speak freely."

"I should defend myself."

"Very good; then I should abandon you here, and what would you do then? You are pretty, you are a woman of sensibility, but many men would take but little account of your virtue. Your lover has left you to me; for all he knew I might be the vilest wretch; but as it is, cheer up, you have nothing to fear.

"How can you think that adventurer loves you? He is a mere monster. I am sorry that what I say makes you weep, but it must be said. I even dare tell you that I have taken a great liking to you; but you may feel quite sure that I shall not ask you to give me so much as a kiss, and I will never abandon you. Before we get to Rome I shall convince you that the count, as he calls himself, not only does not love you, but is a common swindler as well as a deceiver."

"You will convince me of that?"

"Yes, on my word of honour! Dry your eyes, and let us try to make this day pass as pleasantly as yesterday. You cannot imagine how glad I feel that chance has constituted me your protector. I want you to feel assured of my friendship, and if you do not give me a little love in return, I will try and bear it patiently."

The landlord came in and brought the bill for the count and his mistress as well as for myself. I had expected this, and paid it without a word, and without looking at the poor wandering sheep beside me. I recollected that too strong medicines kill, and do not cure, and I was afraid I had said almost too much.

I longed to know her history, and felt sure I should hear it before we reached Rome. We took some coffee and departed, and not a word passed between us till we got to the inn at La Scala, where we got down.

The road from La Scala to Radicofani is steep and troublesome. The vetturino would require an extra horse, and even then would have taken four hours. I decided, therefore, to take two post horses, and not to begin the journey till ten o'clock.

"Would it not be better to go on now?" said the English girl; "it will be very hot from ten till noon."

"Yes, but the Comte de l'Ltoile, whom we should be sure to meet at Radicofani, would not like to see me."

"Why not? I am sure he would."

If I had told her my reason she would have wept anew, so in pity I spared her. I saw that she was blinded by love, and could not see the true character of her lover. It would be impossible to cure her by gentle and persuasive argument; I must speak sharply, the wound must be subjected to the actual cautery. But was virtue the cause of all this interest? Was it devotion to a young and innocent girl that made me willing to undertake so difficult and so delicate a task? Doubtless these motives went for something, but I will not attempt to strut in borrowed plumes, and must freely confess that if she had been ugly and stupid I should probably have left her to her fate. In short, selfishness was at the bottom of it all, so let us say no more about virtue.

My true aim was to snatch this delicate morsel from another's hand that I might enjoy it myself. I did not confess as much to myself, for I could never bear to calmly view my own failings, but afterwards I came to the conclusion that I acted a part throughout. Is selfishness, then, the universal motor of our actions? I am afraid it is.

I made Betty (such was her name) take a country walk with me, and the scenery there is so beautiful that no poet nor painter could imagine a more delicious prospect. Betty spoke Tuscan with English idioms and an English accent, but her voice was so silvery and clear that her Italian was delightful to listen to. I longed to kiss her lips as they spoke so sweetly, but I respected her and restrained myself.

We were walking along engaged in agreeable converse, when all at once we heard the church bells peal out. Betty said she had never seen a Catholic service, and I was glad to give her that pleasure. It was the feast day of some local saint, and Betty assisted at high mass with all propriety, imitating the gestures of the people, so that no one would have taken her for a Protestant. After it was over, she said she thought the Catholic rite was much more adapted to the needs of loving souls than the Angelican. She was astonished at the southern beauty of the village girls, whom she pronounced to be much handsomer that the country lasses in England. She asked me the time, and I replied without thinking that I wondered she had not got a watch. She blushed and said the count had asked her to give it him to leave in pawn for the horse he hired.

I was sorry for what I had said, for I had put Betty, who was incapable of a lie, to great pain.

We started at ten o'clock with three horses, and as a cool wind was blowing we had a pleasant drive, arriving at Radicofani at noon.

The landlord, who was also the postmaster, asked if I would pay three pauls which the Frenchman had expended for his horse and himself, assuring the landlord that his friend would pay.

For Betty's sake I said I would pay; but this was not all.

"The gentleman," added the man, "has beaten three of my postillions with his naked sword. One of them was wounded in the face, and he has followed his assailant, and will make him pay dearly for it. The reason of the assault was that they wanted to detain him till he had paid."

"You were wrong to allow violence to be used; he does not look like a thief, and you might have taken it for granted that I should pay."

"You are mistaken; I was not obliged to take anything of the sort for granted; I have been cheated in this sort many times before. Your dinner is ready if you want any."

Poor Betty was in despair. She observed a distressed silence; and I tried to raise her spirits, and to make her eat a good dinner, and to taste the excellent Muscat, of which the host had provided an enormous flask.

All my efforts were in vain, so I called the vetturino to tell him that I wanted to start directly after dinner. This order acted on Betty like magic.

"You mean to go as far as Centino, I suppose," said the man. "We had better wait there till the heat is over."

"No, we must push on, as the lady's husband may be in need of help. The wounded postillion has followed him; and as he speaks Italian very imperfectly, there's no knowing what may happen to him."

"Very good; we will go off."

Betty looked at me with the utmost gratitude; and by way of proving it, she pretended to have a good appetite. She had noticed that this was a certain way of pleasing me.

While we were at dinner I ordered up one of the beaten postillions, and heard his story. He was a frank rogue; he said he had received some blows with the flat of the sword, but he boasted of having sent a stone after the Frenchman which must have made an impression on him.

I gave him a Paul, and promised to make it a crown if he would go to Centino to bear witness against his comrade, and he immediately began to speak up for the count, much to Betty's amusement. He said the man's wound in the face was a mere scratch, and that he had brought it on himself, as he had no business to oppose a traveller as he had done. By way of comfort he told us that the Frenchman had only been hit by two or three stones. Betty did not find this very consoling, but I saw that the affair was more comic than tragic, and would end in nothing. The postillion went off, and we followed him in half an hour.

Betty was tranquil enough till we got there, and heard that the count had gone on to Acquapendente with the two postillions at his heels; she seemed quite vexed. I told her that all would be well; that the count knew how to defend himself; but she only answered me with a deep sigh.

I suspected that she was afraid we should have to pass the night together, and that I would demand some payment for all the trouble I had taken.

"Would you like us to go on to Acquapendente?" I asked her.

At this question her face beamed all over; she opened her arms, and I embraced her.

I called the vetturino, and told him. I wanted to go on to Acquapendente immediately.

The fellow replied that his horses were in the stable, and that he was not going to put them in; but that I could have post horses if I liked.

"Very good. Get me two horses immediately."

It is my belief that, if I had liked, Betty would have given me everything at that moment, for she let herself fall into my arms. I pressed her tenderly and kissed her, and that was all She seemed grateful for my self-restraint.

The horses were put in, and after I had paid the landlord for the supper, which he swore he had prepared for us, we started.

We reached Acquapendente in three quarters of an hour, and we found the madcap count in high spirits. He embraced his Dulcinea with transports, and Betty seemed delighted to find him safe and sound. He told us triumphantly that he had beaten the rascally postillions, and had warded their stones off.

"Where's the slashed postillion?" I asked.

"He is drinking to my health with his comrade; they have both begged my pardon."

"Yes," said Betty, "this gentleman gave him a crown."

"What a pity! You shouldn't have given them anything."

Before supper the Comte de l'Etoile skewed us the bruises on his thighs and side; the rascal was a fine well-made fellow. However, Betty's adoring airs irritated me, though I was consoled at the thought of the earnest I had received from her.

Next day, the impudent fellow told me that he would order us a good supper at Viterbo, and that of course I would lend him a sequin to pay for his dinner at Montefiascone. So saying, he skewed me in an off-hand way a bill of exchange on Rome for three thousand crowns.

I did not trouble to read it, and gave him the sequin, though I felt sure
I should never see it again.

161

Betty now treated me quite confidentially, and I felt I might ask her almost any questions.

When we were at Montefiascone she said,—

"You see my lover is only without money by chance; he has a bill of exchange for a large amount."

"I believe it to be a forgery."

"You are really too cruel."

"Not at all; I only wish I were mistaken, but I am sure of the contrary. Twenty years ago I should have taken it for a good one, but now it's another thing, and if the bill is a good one, why did he not negotiate it at Sienna, Florence, or Leghorn?"

"It may be that he had not the time; he was in such a hurry to be gone.
Ah! if you knew all!"

"I only want to know what you like to tell me, but I warn you again that what I say is no vague suspicion but hard fact."

"Then you persist in the idea that he does not love me."

"Nay, he loves you, but in such a fashion as to deserve hatred in return."

"How do you mean?"

"Would you not hate a man who loved you only to traffic in your charms?"

"I should be sorry for you to think that of him."

"If you like, I will convince you of what I say this evening."

"You will oblige me; but I must have some positive proof. It would be a sore pain to me, but also a true service."

"And when you are convinced, will you cease to love him?"

"Certainly; if you prove him to be dishonest, my love will vanish away."

"You are mistaken; you will still love him, even when you have had proof positive of his wickedness. He has evidently fascinated you in a deadly manner, or you would see his character in its true light before this."

"All this may be true; but do you give me your proofs, and leave to me the care of shewing that I despise him."

"I will prove my assertions this evening; but tell me how long you have known him?"

"About a month; but we have only been together for five days."

"And before that time you never accorded him any favours?"

"Not a single kiss. He was always under my windows, and I had reason to believe that he loved me fondly."

"Oh, yes! he loves you, who would not? but his love is not that of a man of honour, but that of an impudent profligate."

"But how can you suspect a man of whom you know nothing?"

"Would that I did not know him! I feel sure that not being able to visit you, he made you visit him, and then persuaded you to fly with him."

"Yes, he did. He wrote me a letter, which I will shew you. He promises to marry me at Rome."

"And who is to answer for his constancy?"

"His love is my surety."

"Do you fear pursuit?"

"No."

"Did he take you from a father, a lover, or a brother?"

"From a lover, who will not be back at Leghorn for a week or ten days."

"Where has he gone?"

"To London on business; I was under the charge of a woman whom he trusted."

"That's enough; I pity you, my poor Betty. Tell me if you love your
Englishman, and if he is worthy of your love."

"Alas! I loved him dearly till I saw this Frenchman, who made me unfaithful to a man I adored. He will be in despair at not finding me when he returns."

"Is he rich?"

"Not very; he is a business man, and is comfortably off."

"Is he young?"

"No. He is a man of your age, and a thoroughly kind and honest person. He was waiting for his consumptive wife to die to marry me."

"Poor man! Have you presented him with a child?"

"No. I am sure God did not mean me for him, for the count has conquered me completely."

"Everyone whom love leads astray says the same thing."

"Now you have heard everything, and I am glad I told you, for I am sure you are my friend."

"I will be a better friend to you, dear Betty, in the future than in the past. You will need my services, and I promise not to abandon you. I love you, as I have said; but so long as you continue to love the Frenchman I shall only ask you to consider me as your friend."

"I accept your promise, and in return I promise not to hide anything from you."

"Tell me why you have no luggage."

"I escaped on horseback, but my trunk, which is full of linen and other effects, will be at Rome two days after us. I sent it off the day before my escape, and the man who received it was sent by the count."

"Then good-bye to your trunk!"

"Why, you foresee nothing but misfortune!"

"Well, dear Betty, I only wish my prophecies may not be accomplished. Although you escaped on horseback I think you should have brought a cloak and a carpet bag with some linen."

"All that is in the small trunk; I shall have it taken into my room tonight."

We reached Viterbo at seven o'clock, and found the count very cheerful.

In accordance with the plot I had laid against the count, I began by shewing myself demonstratively fond of Betty, envying the fortunate lover, praising his heroic behaviour in leaving her to me, and so forth.

The silly fellow proceeded to back me up in my extravagant admiration. He boasted that jealousy was utterly foreign to his character, and maintained that the true lover would accustom himself to see his mistress inspire desires in other men.

He proceeded to make a long dissertation on this theme, and I let him go on, for I was waiting till after supper to come to the conclusive point.

During the meal I made him drink, and applauded his freedom from vulgar prejudices. At dessert he enlarged on the duty of reciprocity between lovers.

"Thus," he remarked, "Betty ought to procure me the enjoyment of Fanny, if she has reason to think I have taken a fancy to her; and per contra, as I adore Betty, if I found that she loved you I should procure her the pleasure of sleeping with you."

Betty listened to all this nonsense in silent astonishment.

"I confess, my dear count," I replied, "that, theoretically speaking, your system strikes me as sublime, and calculated to bring about the return of the Golden Age; but I am afraid it would prove absurd in practice. No doubt you are a man of courage, but I am sure you would never let your mistress be enjoyed by another man. Here are twenty-five sequins. I will wager that amount that you will not allow me to sleep with your wife."

"Ha! ha! You are mistaken in me, I assure you. I'll bet fifty sequins that I will remain in the room a calm spectator of your exploits. My dear Betty, we must punish this sceptic; go to bed with him."

"You are joking."

"Not at all; to bed with you, I shall love you all the more."

"You must be crazy, I shall do nothing of the kind."

The count took her in his arms, and caressing her in the tenderest manner begged her to do him this favour, not so much for the twenty-five Louis, as to convince me that he was above vulgar prejudices. His caresses became rather free, but Betty repulsed him gently though firmly, saying that she would never consent, and that he had already won the bet, which was the case; in fine the poor girl besought him to kill her rather than oblige her to do a deed which she thought infamous.

Her words, and the pathetic voice with which they were uttered, should have shamed him, but they only put him into a furious rage. He repulsed her, calling her the vilest names, and finally telling her that she was a hypocrite, and he felt certain she had already granted me all a worthless girl could grant.

Betty grew pale as death, and furious in my turn, I ran for my sword. I should probably have run him through, if the infamous scoundrel had not fled into the next room, where he locked himself in.

I was in despair at seeing Betty's distress, of which I had been the innocent cause, and I did my best to soothe her.

She was in an alarming state. Her breath came with difficulty, her eyes seemed ready to start out of her head, her lips were bloodless and trembling, and her teeth shut tight together. Everyone in the inn was asleep. I could not call for help, and all I could do was to dash water in her face, and speak soothing words.

At last she fell asleep, and I remained beside her for more than two hours, attentive to her least movements, and hoping that she would awake strengthened and refreshed.

At day-break I heard L'Etoile going off, and I was glad of it. The people of the inn knocked at our door, and then Betty awoke.

"Are you ready to go, my dear Betty?"

"I am much better, but I should so like a cup of tea."

The Italians cannot make tea, so I took what she gave me, and went to prepare it myself.

When I came back I found her inhaling the fresh morning air at the window. She seemed calm, and I hoped I had cured her. She drank a few cups of tea (of which beverage the English are very fond), and soon regained her good looks.

She heard some people in the room where we had supped, and asked me if I had taken up the purse which I had placed on the table. I had forgotten it completely.

I found my purse and a piece of paper bearing the words, "bill of exchange for three thousand crowns." The impostor had taken it out of his pocket in making his bet, and had forgotten it. It was dated at Bordeaux, drawn on a wine merchant at Paris to L'Etoile's order. It was payable at sight, and was for six months. The whole thing was utterly irregular.

I took it to Betty, who told me she knew nothing about bills, and begged me to say nothing more about that infamous fellow. She then said, in a voice of which I can give no idea,—

"For pity's sake do not abandon a poor girl, more worthy of compassion than blame!"

I promised her again to have all a father's care for her, and soon after we proceeded on our journey.

The poor girl fell asleep, and I followed her example. We were awoke by the vetturino who informed us, greatly to our astonishment, that we were at Monterosi. We had slept for six hours, and had done eighteen miles.

We had to stay at Monterosi till four o'clock, and we were glad of it, for we needed time for reflection.

In the first place I asked about the wretched deceiver, and was told that he had made a slight meal, paid for it, and said he was going to spend the night at La Storta.

We made a good dinner, and Betty plucking up a spirit said we must consider the case of her infamous betrayer, but for the last time.

"Be a father to me," said she; "do not advise but command; you may reckon on my obedience. I have no need to give you any further particulars, for you have guessed all except the horror with which the thought of my betrayer now inspires me. If it had not been for you, he would have plunged me into an abyss of shame and misery."

"Can you reckon on the Englishman forgiving you?"

"I think so."

"Then we must go back to Leghorn. Are you strong enough to follow this counsel? I warn you that if you approve of it, it must be put into execution at once. Young, pretty, and virtuous as you are, you need not imagine that I shall allow you to go by yourself, or in the company of strangers. If you think I love you, and find me worthy of your esteem, that is sufficient regard for me. I will live with you like a father, if you are not in a position to give me marks of a more ardent affection. Be sure I will keep faith with you, for I want to redeem your opinion of men, and to shew you that there are men as honourable as your seducer was vile."

Betty remained for a quarter of an hour in profound silence, her head resting on her elbows, and her eyes fixed on mine. She did not seem either angry or astonished, but as far as I could judge was lost in thought. I was glad to see her reflective, for thus she would be able to give me a decided answer. At last she said:

"You need not think, my dear friend, that my silence proceeds from irresolution. If my mind were not made up already I should despise myself. I am wise enough at any rate to appreciate the wisdom of your generous counsels. I thank Providence that I have fallen into the hands of such a man who will treat me as if I were his daughter."

"Then we will go back to Leghorn, and start immediately."

"My only doubt is how to manage my reconciliation with Sir B—— M——. I have no doubt he will pardon me eventually; but though he is tender and good-hearted he is delicate where a point of honour is concerned, and subject to sudden fits of violence. This is what I want to avoid; for he might possibly kill me, and then I should be the cause of his ruin."

"You must consider it on the way, and tell me any plans you may think of."

"He is an intelligent man, and it would be hopeless to endeavour to dupe him by a lie. I must make a full confession in writing without hiding a single circumstance; for if he thought he was being duped his fury would be terrible. If you will write to him you must not say that you think me worthy of forgiveness; you must tell him the facts and leave him to judge for himself. He will be convinced of my repentance when he reads the letter I shall bedew with my tears, but he must not know of my whereabouts till he has promised to forgive me. He is a slave to his word of honour, and we shall live together all our days without my ever hearing of this slip. I am only sorry that I have behaved so foolishly."

"You must not be offended if I ask you whether you have ever given him like cause for complaint before."

"Never."

"What is his history?"

"He lived very unhappily with his first wife; and he was divorced from his second wife for sufficient reasons. Two years ago he came to our school with Nancy's father, and made my acquaintance. My father died, his creditors seized everything, and I had to leave the school, much to Nancy's distress and that of the other pupils. At this period Sir B—— M—— took charge of me, and gave me a sum which placed me beyond the reach of, want for the rest of my days. I was grateful, and begged him to take me with him when he told me he was leaving England. He was astonished; and, like a man of honour, said he loved me too well to flatter himself that we could travel together without his entertaining more ardent feelings for me than those of a father. He thought it out of the question for me to love him, save as a daughter.

"This declaration, as you may imagine, paved the way for a full agreement."

"'However you love me,' I said, 'I shall be well pleased, and if I can do anything for you I shall be all the happier.'

"He then gave me of his own free will a written promise to marry me on the death of his wife. We started on our travels, and till my late unhappy connection I never gave him the slightest cause for complaint."

"Dry your eyes, dear Betty, he is sure to forgive you. I have friends at Leghorn, and no one shall find out that we have made acquaintance. I will put you in good hands, and I shall not leave the town till I hear you are back with Sir B—— M——. If he prove inexorable I promise never to abandon you, and to take you back to England if you like."

"But how can you spare the time?"

"I will tell you the truth, my dear Betty. I have nothing particular to do at Rome, or anywhere else. London and Rome are alike to me."

"How can I shew my gratitude to you?"

I summoned the vetturino, and told him we must return to Viterbo. He objected, but I convinced him with a couple of piastres, and by agreeing to use the post horses and to spare his own animals.

We got to Viterbo by seven o'clock, and asked anxiously if no one had found a pocket-book which I pretended I had lost. I was told no such thing had been found, so I ordered supper with calmness, although bewailing my loss. I told Betty that I acted in this sort to obviate any difficulties which the vetturino might make about taking us back to Sienna, as he might feel it his duty to place her in the hands of her supposed husband. I had up the small trunk, and after we had forced the lock Betty took out her cloak and the few effects she had in it, and we then inspected the adventurer's properties, most likely all he possessed in the world. A few tattered shirts, two or three pairs of mended silk stockings, a pair of breeches, a hare's foot, a pot of grease, and a score of little books- plays or comic operas, and lastly a packet of letters; such were the contents of the trunk.

We proceeded to read the letters, and the first thing we noted was the address: "To M. L'Etoile, Actor, at Marseilles, Bordeaux, Bayonne, Montpellier, etc."

I pitied Betty. She saw herself the dupe of a vile actor, and her indignation and shame were great.

"We will read it all to-morrow," said I; "to-day we have something else to do."

The poor girl seemed to breathe again.

We got over our supper hastily, and then Betty begged me to leave her alone for a few moments for her to change her linen and go to bed.

"If you like," said I, "I will have a bed made up for me in the next room."

"No, dear friend, ought I not to love your society? What would have become of me without you?"

I went out for a few minutes, and when I returned and came to her bedside to wish her good night, she gave me such a warm embrace that I knew my hour was come.

Reader, you must take the rest for granted. I was happy, and I had reason to believe that Betty was happy also.

In the morning, we had just fallen asleep, when the vetturino knocked at the door.

I dressed myself hastily to see him.

"Listen," I said, "it is absolutely necessary for me to recover my pocket-book, and I hope to find it at Acquapendente."

"Very good, sir, very good," said the rogue, a true Italian, "pay me as if I had taken you to Rome, and a sequin a day for the future, and if you like, I will take you to England on those terms."

The vetturino was evidently what is called wide awake. I gave him his

money, and we made a new agreement. At seven o'clock we stopped at

Montefiascone to write to Sir B—— M——, she in English, and I in

French.

Betty had now an air of satisfaction and assurance which I found charming. She said she was full of hope, and seemed highly amused at the thought of the figure which the actor would cut when he arrived at Rome by himself. She hoped that we should come across the man in charge of her trunk, and that we should have no difficulty in getting it back.

"He might pursue us."

"He dare not do so."

"I expect not, but if he does I will give him a warm welcome. If he does not take himself off I will blow out his brains."

Before I began my letter to Sir B—— M——. Betty again warned me to conceal nothing from him.

"Not even the reward you gave me?"

"Oh, yes! That is a little secret between ourselves."

In less than three hours the letters were composed and written. Betty was satisfied with my letter; and her own, which she translated for my benefit, was a perfect masterpiece of sensibility, which seemed to me certain of success.

I thought of posting from Sienna, to ensure her being in a place of safety before the arrival of her lover.

The only thing that troubled me was the bill of exchange left behind by L'Etoile, for whether it were true or false, I felt bound to deal with it in some way, but I could not see how it was to be done.

We set out again after dinner in spite of the heat, and arrived at Acquapendente in the evening and spent the night in the delights of mutual love.

As I was getting up in the morning I saw a carriage in front of the inn, just starting for Rome. I imagined that amidst the baggage Betty's trunk might be discovered, and I told her to get up, and see if it were there. We went down, and Betty recognized the trunk she had confided to her seducer.

We begged the vetturino to restore it to us, but he was inflexible; and as he was in the right we had to submit. The only thing he could do was to have an embargo laid on the trunk at Rome, the said embargo to last for a month. A notary was called, and our claim properly drawn up. The vetturino, who seemed an honest and intelligent fellow, assured us he had received nothing else belonging to the Comte de L'Etoile, so we were assured that the actor was a mere beggar on the lookout for pickings, and that the rags in the small trunk were all his possessions.

After this business had been dispatched Betty brightened up amazingly.

"Heaven," she exclaimed, "is arranging everything. My mistake will serve as a warning to me for the future, for the lesson has been a severe one, and might have been much worse if I had not had the good fortune of meeting you."

"I congratulate you," I replied, "on having cured yourself so quickly of a passion that had deprived you of your reason."

"Ah! a woman's reason is a fragile thing. I shudder when I think of the monster; but I verily believe that I should not have regained my senses if he had not called me a hypocrite, and said that he was certain I had already granted you my favours. These infamous words opened my eyes, and made me see my shame. I believe I would have helped you to pierce him to the heart if the coward had not run away. But I am glad he did run away, not for his sake but for ours, for we should have been in an unpleasant position if he had been killed."

"You are right; he escaped my sword because he is destined for the rope."

"Let him look to that himself, but I am sure he will never dare to shew his face before you or me again."

We reached Radicofani at ten o'clock, and proceeded to write postscripts to our letters to Sir B—— M—— We were sitting at the same table, Betty opposite to the door and I close to it, so that anyone coming in could not have seen me without turning round.

Betty was dressed with all decency and neatness, but I had taken off my coat on account of the suffocating heat. Nevertheless, though I was in shirt sleeves, I should not have been ashamed of my attire before the most respectable woman in Italy.

All at once I heard a rapid step coming along the passage, and the door was dashed open. A furious-looking man came in, and, seeing Betty, cried out,—

"Ah! there you are."

I did not give him time to turn round and see me, but leapt upon him and seized him by the shoulders. If I had not done so he would have shot me dead on the spot.

As I leapt upon him I had involuntarily closed the door, and as he cried,
"Let me go, traitor!" Betty fell on her knees before him, exclaiming, "No, no! he is my preserver."

Sir B—— M—— was too mad with rage to pay any attention to her, and kept on,—-

"Let me go, traitors!"

As may be imagined, I did not pay much attention to this request so long as the loaded pistol was in his hand.

In our struggles he at last fell to the ground and I on top of him. The landlord and his people had heard the uproar, and were trying to get in; but as we had fallen against the door they could not do so.

Betty had the presence of mind to snatch the pistol from his hand, and I then let him go, calmly observing,

"Sir, you are labouring under a delusion."

Again Betty threw herself on her knees, begging him to calm himself, as I was her preserver not her betrayer.

"What do you mean by 'preserver'?" said B—— M——

Betty gave him the letter, saying,—

"Read that."

The Englishman read the letter through without rising from the ground, and as I was certain of its effect I opened the door and told the landlord to send his people away, and to get dinner for three, as everything had been settled.

The End

www.ingramcontent.com/pod-product-compliance
Lightning Source LLC
Chambersburg PA
CBHW070010300526
45794CB00001B/261